ألف ليلة وليلة

لمتعلمي اللغة العربية
(المستوى المتوسط)

One Thousand and One Nights

for Intermediate Arabic
Language Learners

lingualism

© 2023 by Matthew Aldrich

The author's moral rights have been asserted. All rights reserved. No part of this document may be reproduced or transmitted in any form or by any means, electronic, mechanical, photocopying, recording, or otherwise, without prior written permission of the publisher.

ISBN: 978-1-949650-95-2

Conceptualized by Matthew Aldrich

Written by Ahmad Al-Masri

Edited by Hend Khaled and Matthew Aldrich

Illustrations by Duc-Minh Vu

Audio by Mohamed Shehata

website: www.lingualism.com

email: contact@lingualism.com

Table of Contents

II .... INTRODUCTION

V .... HOW TO USE THIS BOOK

1 .... الفَصْلُ الأوَّلُ: المَلِكُ شَهْرِيارُ والوزيرُ وابْنَتُهُ شَهْرَزادُ

Chapter 1: King Shahryar, the Vizier, and his Daughter Scheherazade

11 .... الفَصْلُ الثّاني: قِصَّةُ التّاجِرِ والجِنِّيِّ

Chapter 2: The Tale of the Merchant and the Genie

23 .... الفَصْلُ الثّالِثُ: الصَّيّادُ والسَّمَكَةُ الذَّهَبِيَّةُ

Chapter 3: The Fisherman and the Golden Fish

33 .... الفَصْلُ الرّابِعُ: عَلاءُ الدّينِ والْمِصْباحُ السِّحْرِيُّ

Chapter 4: Aladdin and the Magic Lamp

44 .... الفَصْلُ الخامِسُ: عَلي بابا والأرْبَعونَ لِصًّا

Chapter 5: Ali Baba and the Forty Thieves

54 .... الفَصْلُ السّادِسُ: الفَلّاحُ الذَّكِيُّ والجِنِّيُّ المُشاغِبُ

Chapter 6: The Clever Farmer and the Mischievous Genie

64 .... الفَصْلُ السّابِعُ: لِصُّ الإسْكَنْدَرِيَّةِ وَرَئيسُ الشُّرْطَةِ

Chapter 7: The Thief of Alexandria and the Police Chief

75 .... الفَصْلُ الثّامِنُ: الطّائِرُ الأزْرَقُ

Chapter 8: The Blue Bird

86 .... الفَصْلُ التّاسِعُ: الفَتاةُ والسّاحِرَةُ

Chapter 9: The Girl and the Sorceress

96 .... الفَصْلُ العاشِرُ: الأميرُ والتِّنّينُ

Chapter 10: The Prince and the Dragon

Introduction

"One Thousand and One Nights for Intermediate Arabic Language Learners" is a captivating anthology designed specifically for adult **Modern Standard Arabic** language learners at the intermediate (B1-B2) level. This unique collection features the cherished classic tales in a simplified, yet engaging format, making it an excellent resource for those venturing into the enchanting world of Arabic language and literature.

The book comes with an array of special features to ensure an immersive and effective learning experience:

- **Diacritics for Pronunciation:** We've included diacritical marks (tashkeel) in the Arabic text to assist you in correct pronunciation, and to clarify the meaning of the words, easing your reading experience.

- **Professional Audio Accompaniment:** The book is supplemented with high-quality, slow-paced audio readings by a professional voice artist who is a native Arabic speaker. This allows you to listen and mimic the correct pronunciation, intonation, and rhythm of Arabic.

- **Comprehension Questions and Answers:** Each chapter is followed by a set of comprehension questions, along with their answers. This interactive feature helps to reinforce your understanding of the story and the language constructs used within it.

- **English Translations:** To support your learning, we've provided English translations of the stories. These can be used as a reference to cross-check your understanding of the Arabic text.

All these features work together to provide a comprehensive and enriching learning experience, ensuring you make consistent progress in your Arabic language journey.

The tales in this book have been carefully curated and reimagined to match the language proficiency of intermediate-level learners. We have incorporated level-appropriate vocabulary throughout the stories, ensuring you are neither overwhelmed by complexity nor left unchallenged. To enhance memorization and recognition, we've deliberately woven repetitive patterns of phrases and language structures into the text, encouraging natural language acquisition and recall.

Each chapter is short, and perfectly crafted to be absorbed in a single sitting, allowing you to steadily build your comprehension skills and vocabulary without feeling rushed. The stories retain the intrigue and charm of the original tales, providing you with a sense of accomplishment and enjoyment as you navigate your way through each tale.

As you delve into the enriched narratives found in "One Thousand and One Nights for Intermediate Arabic Language Learners," you might notice an escalation in language complexity. If at any point the text appears too formidable, we would highly recommend you to revisit "One Thousand and One Nights for Elementary Arabic Language Learners." The elementary-level book is meticulously designed to provide you with a firm grounding in the most common vocabulary used in the stories and acquaints you with straightforward sentence structures. Spending adequate time with the elementary book can help you grasp the fundamentals of the language effectively. Once you have a solid foundation and feel comfortable with the elementary material, we encourage you to return to the intermediate version. By then, the expanded vocabulary and more advanced sentence structures will no longer seem as daunting but will instead present a rewarding and manageable challenge, fostering your seamless progression towards mastery in Arabic.

How to Use This Book

"One Thousand and One Nights for Intermediate Arabic Language Learners" has been designed to offer flexibility to adapt to your individual learning style. Here's how you can utilize the features of the book according to your needs:

1. **Choose Your Approach:** You have the freedom to approach the stories in multiple ways. You could begin by tackling the Arabic text first, immersing yourself in the structure of the language and the flow of the story. Alternatively, you could start by listening to the accompanying audio, to attune your ear to the sound and rhythm of Arabic. This can be particularly helpful if you are a more auditory learner.

2. **Use English Translations:** If you're finding the Arabic text or audio challenging, you can refer to the English translations to aid your understanding. Over time, as your comprehension improves, you could challenge yourself by attempting to read or listen to the Arabic without relying on the translations.

3. **Engage with Questions:** You can choose to tackle the comprehension questions before or after reading the story. Attempting them beforehand can provide a focus for your reading, while answering them after

allows you to assess your understanding of the text. Remember, the answers provided in the book are examples and your own answers, while differently worded, may still be correct.

4. **Repetition and Practice:** This book has been designed to promote repetition and practice, key strategies for language learning. We encourage you to revisit chapters and listen to the audio multiple times to reinforce your understanding and memorization.

Remember, the most effective learning strategy is the one that works best for you. So don't be afraid to experiment with different approaches until you find what suits you best.

Visit www.lingualism.com/audio, where you can find the free accompanying audio to download or stream (at variable playback rates).

الفَصْلُ الأَوَّلُ
المَلِكُ شَهْرَيارُ وَالوَزيرُ وَابْنَتُهُ شَهْرَزاد

في قَديمِ الزَّمانِ، كانَ هُناكَ مَلِكٌ يُدْعى شَهْرَيارُ يَحْكُمُ مَمْلَكَةً واسِعَةً وَغَنِيَّةً. كانَ المَلِكُ شَهْرَيارُ يَعْتَمِدُ عَلى وَزيرِهِ الأَمينِ الذَّكِيِّ في إِدارَةِ شُؤُونِ المَمْلَكَةِ. كانَ لِلْوَزيرِ ابْنَةٌ جَميلَةٌ وَذَكِيَّةٌ تُدْعى شَهْرَزادَ، وَكانَتْ مَشْهورَةً بِذَكائِها الفَريدِ وَمَعْرِفَتِها الواسِعَةِ

بِالقِصَصِ وَالتَّارِيخِ.

ذَاتَ يَوْمٍ، عَلِمَ المَلِكُ شَهْرَيارُ بِخِيانَةِ زَوْجَتِهِ لَهُ، فَشَعَرَ بِالغَضَبِ وَالحُزْنِ الشَّدِيدِ. قَرَّرَ شَهْرَيارُ أَنْ يَتَزَوَّجَ مِنَ امْرَأَةٍ جَدِيدَةٍ كُلَّ لَيْلَةٍ وَيَقْتُلَها فِي الصَّباحِ التَّالِي حَتَّى لا تَتَسَنَّى لَها الفُرْصَةُ لِخِيانَتِهِ. كانَ سُلُوكُ المَلِكِ شَهْرَيارَ هَذا يُسَبِّبُ الرُّعْبَ وَالفَزَعَ بَيْنَ نِساءِ وَأَهالِي المَمْلَكَةِ.

أَدْرَكَتْ شَهْرَزادُ أَنَّها يَجِبُ أَنْ تَتَدَخَّلَ لِإِنْقاذِ نِساءِ المَمْلَكَةِ وَإِعادَةِ الأَمَلِ لِشَعْبِها. اِقْتَرَحَتْ عَلَى وَالِدِها الوَزِيرِ أَنْ تَتَزَوَّجَ مِنَ المَلِكِ شَهْرَيارَ. رَغْمَ قَلَقِهِ وَخَوْفِهِ عَلَى ابْنَتِهِ، وافَقَ الوَزِيرُ عَلَى مَطْلَبِها بِسَبَبِ ثِقَتِهِ بِذَكائِها وَحِكْمَتِها. قَبْلَ الزِّفافِ، قامَتْ شَهْرَزادُ بِوَضْعِ خُطَّةٍ لِإِقْناعِ المَلِكِ بِالتَّوَقُّفِ عَنْ قَتْلِ النِّساءِ.

فِي لَيْلَةِ زِفافِها، طَلَبَتْ شَهْرَزادُ مِنْ أُخْتِها دِينازادَ أَنْ تَأْتِيَ مَعَها إِلَى قَصْرِ المَلِكِ. كانَتْ دِينازادُ تَعْرِفُ أَمْرَ خُطَّةِ شَهْرَزادَ وَكانَتْ تَعْلَمُ أَنَّ دَوْرَها يَتَمَثَّلُ فِي مُساعَدَتِها وَدَعْمِها. قَبْلَ النَّوْمِ، طَلَبَتْ شَهْرَزادُ

مِنْ دينازادَ أَنْ تَطْلُبَ مِنها سَرْدَ قِصَّةٍ. بَدَأَتْ شَهْرَزادُ بِسَرْدِ قِصَّةٍ رائِعَةٍ وَمُثيرَةٍ لِلاهْتِمامِ لِلْمَلِكِ شَهْرَيارَ. وَتَوَقَّفَتْ عِنْدَ الْمُنْتَصَفِ، قَبْلَ أَنْ يَغْلِبَ النَّوْمُ المَلِكَ. كانَ دَوْرُ دينازادَ الأَساسِيُّ هُوَ تَذْكيرُ شَهْرَزادَ بِبَدْءِ القِصَّةِ وَإِبْداءِ الاِهْتِمامِ بِالاِسْتِماعِ لَها، مِمّا يَجْعَلُ المَلِكَ يَشْعُرُ بِالْفُضولِ وَيَرْغَبُ في الاِسْتِماعِ لِلْقِصَّةِ أَيْضًا.

في الصَّباحِ التّالي، كانَ المَلِكُ شَهْرَيارُ يَتوقُ لِسَماعِ باقي القِصَّةِ. قَرَّرَ عَدَمَ قَتْلِ شَهْرَزادَ وَمَنْحَها فُرْصَةً لِإِتْمامِ القِصَّةِ في اللَّيْلَةِ التّالِيَةِ. لَكِنَّ شَهْرَزادَ عَلِمَتْ أَنَّها لا بُدَّ أَنْ تَكونَ حَكيمَةً وَتَجْعَلَ كُلَّ قِصَّةٍ تَدومُ أَكْثَرَ مِنْ لَيْلَةٍ واحِدَةٍ لِتَضْمَنَ حَياتَها.

في اللَّيْلَةِ الثّانِيَةِ، أَكْمَلَتْ شَهْرَزادُ القِصَّةَ الَّتي بَدَأَتْها، وَبَدَأَتْ قِصَّةً جَديدَةً أَيْضًا. عَلى مَدارِ اللَّيالي التّالِيَةِ، اسْتَمَرَّتْ شَهْرَزادُ في سَرْدِ القِصَصِ المُثيرَةِ وَالشَّيِّقَةِ الَّتي تَتَضَمَّنُ الحِكْمَةَ وَالعِبَرَ، مِمّا أَذْهَلَ المَلِكَ شَهْرَيارَ بِذَكائِها وَثَقافَتِها.

كُلَّ لَيْلَةٍ، كانَتْ دينازادُ تَلْعَبُ دَوْرًا حَيَوِيًّا في تَحْميسِ الأَجْواءِ وَبَدْءِ القِصَصِ. كانَتْ تَظَلُّ مُسْتَيْقِظَةً وَتَسْتَمِعُ لِشَهْرَزادَ بِانْتِباهٍ، مِمّا يُثيرُ

فُضولَ المَلِكِ وَيُحَفِّزُهُ عَلى الاسْتِماعِ لِكُلِّ كَلِمَةٍ تَنْطِقُها.

في اللَّيْلَةِ الأولى مِنْ تِلْكَ الرِّحْلَةِ الطَّويلَةِ مِنَ القِصَصِ وَالحِكاياتِ، بَدَأَتْ شَهْرَزادُ تَرْوي قِصَّةً لِلْمَلِكِ شَهْرَيارَ، قِصَّةً مَليئَةً بِالإثارَةِ وَالمُغامَرَةِ وَالحِكْمَةِ. وَهَكَذا انْطَلَقَتْ رِحْلَةُ شَهْرَزادَ الشُّجاعَةُ وَالحَكيمَةُ لِإنْقاذِ نِساءِ المَمْلَكَةِ وَإعادَةِ الأَمانِ وَالسَّلامِ إلى شَعْبِها.

Questions

1. ما هِيَ مُشْكِلَةُ المَلِكِ شَهْرَيارَ الَّتي أَثَّرَتْ عَلى نِساءِ المَمْلَكَةِ؟

2. ما هِيَ خُطَّةُ شَهْرَزادَ لِإِنْقاذِ نِساءِ المَمْلَكَةِ؟

3. كَيْفَ ساعَدَتْ أُخْتُ شَهْرَزادَ، دينازادُ، في تَنْفيذِ الخُطَّةِ؟

4. ماذا قَرَّرَ المَلِكُ شَهْرَيارُ بَعْدَ سَماعِهِ لِأولى قِصَصِ شَهْرَزادَ؟

5. ما الهَدَفُ مِنْ جَعْلِ كُلِّ قِصَّةٍ تَدومُ أَكْثَرَ مِنْ لَيْلَةٍ واحِدَةٍ؟

Answers

1. مُشْكِلَةُ المَلِكِ شَهْرَيَار كانَتْ غَضَبَهُ مِنْ خِيانَةِ زَوْجَتِهِ لَهُ، وَقَرارَهُ بِالزَّواجِ مِنَ امْرَأَةٍ جَديدَةٍ كُلَّ لَيْلَةٍ وَقَتْلِها في الصَّباحِ التّالي.

2. خُطَّةُ شَهْرَزادَ هِيَ أَنْ تَتَزَوَّجَ مِنَ المَلِكِ شَهْرَيَار وَتَسْرِدَ قِصَصًا مُثيرَةً وَشَيِّقَةً لَهُ كُلَّ لَيْلَةٍ لِيَتَوَقَّفَ عَنْ قَتْلِ النِّساءِ.

3. ساعَدَتْ دينازاد شَهْرَزادَ مِنْ خِلالِ تَذْكيرِها بِبَدْءِ القِصَّةِ وَإِبْداءِ الاِهْتِمامِ بِالاِسْتِماعِ لَها، مِمّا جَعَلَ المَلِكَ يَشْعُرُ بِالفُضولِ وَيَرْغَبُ في الاِسْتِماعِ لِلْقِصَّةِ أَيْضًا.

4. قَرَّرَ المَلِكُ شَهْرَيَار عَدَمَ قَتْلِ شَهْرَزادَ وَمَنَحَها فُرْصَةً لِإِتْمامِ القِصَّةِ في اللَّيْلَةِ التّالِيَةِ.

5. الهَدَفُ مِنْ جَعْلِ كُلِّ قِصَّةٍ تَدومُ أَكْثَرَ مِنْ لَيْلَةٍ واحِدَةٍ هُوَ ضَمانُ حَياةِ شَهْرَزادَ وَإِعْطائِها الوَقْتَ الكافِيَ لِإِقْناعِ المَلِكِ بِالتَّوَقُّفِ عَنْ قَتْلِ النِّساءِ.

Chapter 1: King Shahryar, the Vizier, and his Daughter Scheherazade

In ancient times, a king called Shahryar ruled a vast and rich kingdom. King Shahryar relied on his trustworthy and intelligent vizier to manage the affairs of the kingdom. The vizier had a beautiful and clever daughter named Scheherazade, who was renowned for her exceptional intelligence and wide knowledge of stories and history.

One day, King Shahryar learned of his wife's infidelity, which filled him with great anger and sorrow. He decided to marry a new woman every night and kill her in the morning so that she wouldn't have the chance to betray him. This behavior of King Shahryar caused terror and panic among the women and people of the kingdom.

Scheherazade realized that she must intervene to save the women of the kingdom and restore hope to her people. She proposed to her father, the vizier, that she marry King Shahryar. Despite his concern and fear for his daughter, the vizier agreed to her request due to his trust in her intelligence and wisdom. Before the wedding, Scheherazade devised a plan to convince the king to stop killing the women.

On her wedding night, Scheherazade asked her sister, Dinarzad, to come with her to the palace of the king. Dinarzad knew of Scheherazade's plan and understood that her role was to assist and support her. Before sleep,

Scheherazade asked Dinarzad to request a story from her. Scheherazade began telling a fascinating and interesting story to King Shahryar and stopped in the middle before the king fell asleep. Dinarzad's main role was to remind Scheherazade to start the story and show interest in listening, which made the king curious and eager to hear the story as well.

The next morning, King Shahryar longed to hear the rest of the story. He decided not to kill Scheherazade and gave her a chance to finish the story the next night. But Scheherazade knew that she must be wise and make each story last more than one night to ensure her life.

On the second night, Scheherazade finished the story she began and started a new one. Over the following nights, Scheherazade continued telling thrilling and captivating stories that contained wisdom and morals, which astonished King Shahryar with her intelligence and culture.

Every night, Dinarzad played a vital role in enlivening the atmosphere and starting the stories. She remained awake and listened attentively to Scheherazade, which aroused the king's curiosity and motivated him to listen to every word uttered.

On the first night of this long journey of tales and stories, Scheherazade began telling a story to King Shahryar, a story full of excitement, adventure, and wisdom. And so began the brave and wise journey of Scheherazade to save the women of the kingdom and restore safety and peace to her people.

Questions

1. What was King Shahryar's problem that affected the women of the kingdom?
2. What was Scheherazade's plan to save the women of the kingdom?
3. How did Scheherazade's sister, Dinarzad, help execute the plan?
4. What did King Shahryar decide after hearing Scheherazade's first story?
5. What was the goal of making each story last more than one night?

Answers

1. King Shahryar's problem was his anger over his wife's infidelity and his decision to marry a new woman every night and kill her in the morning.
2. Scheherazade's plan was to marry King Shahryar and tell him thrilling and captivating stories every night to make him stop killing women.
3. Dinarzad helped Scheherazade by reminding her to start the story and show interest in listening, which made the king curious and eager to hear the story as well.

4. King Shahryar decided not to kill Scheherazade and gave her a chance to finish the story the next night.

5. The goal of making each story last more than one night was to ensure Scheherazade's life and give her enough time to convince the king to stop killing women.

الفَصْلُ الثّاني
قِصَّةُ التّاجِرِ وَالجِنِّيِّ

في اللَّيْلَةِ الثّانِيَةِ مِنْ قِصَصِ شَهْرَزادَ، بَدَأَتْ بِرِوايَةِ قِصَّةٍ عَنْ تاجِرٍ ثَرِيٍّ وجِنِّيٍّ عَظيمِ القُوَّةِ. في أَحَدِ الأَيّامِ، قَرَّرَ التّاجِرُ السَّفَرَ إلى مَدينَةٍ بَعيدَةٍ لِبَيْعٍ بِضائِعِهِ. قَبْلَ أَنْ يَبْدَأَ رِحْلَتَهُ، تَوَقَّفَ في غابَةٍ هادِئَةٍ لِيَأْخُذَ قِسْطًا مِنَ الرّاحَةِ وَيَتَناوَلَ طَعامَهُ.

في الغابةِ، قَطَعَ التَّاجِرُ غُصْنَ شَجَرَةٍ لِإشْعالِ نارٍ وَتَسْخينِ طَعامِهِ. لَكِنْ فَجْأَةً، ظَهَرَ جِنِّيٌّ عَظيمُ القُوَّةِ وَالغَضَبِ أمامَ التَّاجِرِ وَصَرَخَ قائِلًا: "أَيُّها الإنسانُ، لَقَدْ قَطَعْتَ غُصْنَ الشَّجَرَةِ الَّتي كانَتْ مَأْوًى لي، وَلِهَذا سَأَقْتُلُكَ!"

أُصيبَ التَّاجِرُ بِالرُّعْبِ وَالذُّعْرِ، وَبَدَأَ يَتَوَسَّلُ لِلْجِنِّيِّ لِيُسامِحَهُ وَيَتْرُكَهُ يَعيشُ. قالَ لِلْجِنِّيِّ إنَّهُ يَمْتَلِكُ عائِلَةً وَأَصْدِقاءَ يَعْتَمِدونَ عَلَيْهِ وَأَنَّهُمْ سَيَموتونَ مِنَ الحُزْنِ إذا فَقَدوهُ. اِسْتَمَعَ الجِنِّيُّ لِلتَّاجِرِ وَقَرَّرَ أَنْ يَمْنَحَهُ فُرْصَةً لِلْتَكْفيرِ عَنْ خَطَئِهِ.

وَعَدَ الجِنِّيُّ التَّاجِرَ بِأَنَّهُ سَيَسْمَحُ لَهُ بِالْعَوْدَةِ إلى عائِلَتِهِ لِمُدَّةِ عامٍ واحِدٍ لِيُوَدِّعَهُمْ وَيَدْفَعَ دُيونَهُ، وَلَكِنْ بِشَرْطِ أَنْ يَعودَ بَعْدَ مُرورِ العامِ لِيَقْتُلَهُ. وافَقَ التَّاجِرُ على الشَّرْطِ وَعادَ إلى مَدينَتِهِ بِقَلْبٍ مُثْقَلٍ بِالْحُزْنِ وَالْخَوْفِ.

عِنْدَ انْتِهاءِ العامِ، بَدَأَ التَّاجِرُ رِحْلَةَ العَوْدَةِ إلى الغابَةِ لِيُواجِهَ مَصيرَهُ المَحْتومَ. وَفي الطَّريقِ، قابَلَ رَجُلًا عَجوزًا يَحْمِلُ عَصًا طَويلَةً. بَدَأَ التَّاجِرُ يَروي لِلْعَجوزِ قِصَّتَهُ مَعَ الجِنِّيِّ وَعَنِ الوَعْدِ الَّذي قَطَعَهُ

لَهُ. أَظْهَرَ العَجوزُ تَعاطُفَهُ مَعَ التَّاجِرِ وَقَرَّرَ مُرافَقَتَهُ إِلى الغابَةِ.

عِنْدَ مُواصَلَتِهِما الرِّحْلَةَ، الْتَقى التّاجِرُ وَالعَجوزُ بِرَجُلَيْنِ آخَرَيْنِ: أَحَدُهُما يَحْمِلُ جَرَّةَ ماءٍ وَالآخَرُ يُمْسِكُ حَبْلًا طَويلًا. انْضَمَّ الرَّجُلانِ إِلى التّاجِرِ وَالعَجوزِ وَتَوَجَّهَ الجَميعُ إِلى الغابَةِ لِمُواجَهَةِ الجِنِّيِّ.

عِنْدَ وُصولِهِمْ إِلى الغابَةِ، ظَهَرَ الجِنِّيُّ وَهَدَّدَ بِقَتْلِ التّاجِرِ. تَدَخَّلَ العَجوزُ وَسَأَلَ الجِنِّيَّ إِذا كانَ يَسْمَحُ لَهُ بِأَنْ يَسْأَلَ ثَلاثَةَ أَسْئِلَةٍ قَبْلَ أَنْ يَقْتُلَ التّاجِرَ. وافَقَ الجِنِّيُّ عَلى طَلَبِ العَجوزِ.

طَرَحَ العَجوزُ السُّؤالَ الأَوَّلَ عَنْ نَفْسِهِ: "كَيْفَ اسْتَطاعَتِ العَصا الطَّويلَةُ أَنْ تَجْلِبَ لِيَ الفائِدَةَ؟" ثُمَّ أَجابَ بِأَنَّهُ اسْتَخْدَمَها لِقِياسِ عُمْقِ النَّهْرِ قَبْلَ عُبورِهِ لِضَمانِ سَلامَتِهِ. ثُمَّ طَرَحَ العَجوزُ السُّؤالَ الثّاني: "ما فائِدَةُ الجَرَّةِ؟" فَأَجابَ الرَّجُلُ الَّذي يَحْمِلُ الجَرَّةَ بِأَنَّهُ يَسْتَخْدِمُها لِحِفْظِ الماءِ وَيُمْكِنُهُ أَنْ يُطْفِئَ بِها النّارَ في حالِ انْدِلاعِ حَريقٍ. أَخيرًا، طَرَحَ العَجوزُ السُّؤالَ الثّالِثَ: "لِماذا تَحْمِلُ الحَبْلَ

الطَّويلَ؟" فَأَجابَ الرَّجُلُ الثّالِثُ بِأَنَّهُ يَسْتَخْدِمُ الحَبْلَ لِيَتَسَلَّقَ الجِبالَ وَيُمْكِنُهُ اسْتِخْدامُهُ لِيُنْقِذَ حَياةَ النّاسِ المُحْتَجَزينَ عَلى قِمَمِها.

عَلى ضَوْءِ إِجاباتِ الأَسْئِلَةِ الثَّلاثَةِ، قالَ العَجوزُ لِلْجِنِّيِّ: "لَقَدِ اسْتَخْدَمَ ثَلاثَتُنا هَذِهِ الأَدَواتِ لِلْمُساعَدَةِ وَالنَّجاةِ، مِمّا يُعَلِّمُنا أَنَّ الحَياةَ قَيِّمَةٌ وَيَجِبُ أَنْ نَسْتَخْدِمَ ما بَيْنَ أَيْدينا لِلْعَيْشِ بِسَلامٍ وَتَعاوُنٍ. أَلَمْ تَعْتَبِرْ يا جِنِّيُّ؟" تَأَثَّرَ الجِنِّيُّ بِكَلِماتِ العَجوزِ وَقَرَّرَ أَنْ يَتْرُكَ التّاجِرَ حَيًّا وَيَعْفُوَ عَنْهُ.

بَعْدَ هَذِهِ التَّجْرِبَةِ المُرَوِّعَةِ وَالصَّعْبَةِ، عادَ التّاجِرُ إِلى مَدينَتِهِ وَشَكَرَ الرِّجالَ الثَّلاثَةَ عَلى مُساعَدَتِهِمْ وَتَضْحِيَتِهِمْ. عَلى الرَّغْمِ مِنْ خَوْفِهِ وَالتَّوَتُّرِ الَّذي مَرَّ بِهِ، تَعَلَّمَ التّاجِرُ قيمَةَ التَّعاوُنِ وَالصَّداقَةِ، وَأَنَّ الحَياةَ تَحْمِلُ الكَثيرَ مِنَ العِبَرِ وَالحِكْمَةِ.

في هَذِهِ الأَثْناءِ، اسْتَمَعَ المَلِكُ شَهْرَيارُ بِشَغَفٍ إِلى قِصَّةِ شَهْرَزادَ. بَدَأَ يَتَعَلَّقُ بِشَخْصِيّاتِ القِصَّةِ وَيَتَعاطَفُ مَعَ مَشاعِرِهِمْ وَمُعاناتِهِمْ. وَبِفَضْلِ هَذِهِ القِصَّةِ، بَدَأَ المَلِكُ يَرى الحَياةَ بِعُيونٍ جَديدَةٍ وَيُدْرِكُ

أَنَّ النّاسَ يُمْكِنُهُمْ أَنْ يَتَغَيَّروا، وَأَنَّ الحِكْمَةَ وَالعِبَرَ تَأْتي مِنَ التَّجارِبِ المُخْتَلِفَةِ.

في اللَّيْلَةِ التّالِيَةِ، انْتَهَتْ شَهْرَزادُ مِنْ رِوايَةِ قِصَّةِ التّاجِرِ وَالجِنِّيِّ وَبَدَأَتْ في سَرْدِ قِصَّةٍ جَديدَةٍ. وَعَلى هَذا المِنْوالِ اسْتَمَرَّتْ شَهْرَزادُ في تَأْسيسِ الثِّقَةِ بَيْنَها وَبَيْنَ المَلِكِ شَهْرَيار وَعَلَّمَتْهُ دُروسًا ثَمينَةً عَنِ الحُبِّ وَالإِنْسانِيَّةِ وَالعَدْلِ مِنْ خِلالِ القِصَصِ الرّائِعَةِ وَالمَليئَةِ بِالحِكْمَةِ.

وَمَعَ كُلِّ قِصَّةٍ تَرْويها شَهْرَزادُ، كانَتْ دينازادُ دائِمًا إلى جانِبِها وَتَقومُ بِدَوْرِها في جَعْلِ المَلِكِ مُهْتَمًّا وَمُتَشَوِّقًا لِسَماعِ المَزيدِ. وَبِذَلِكَ، كانَتْ شَهْرَزادُ تُنْقِذُ نَفْسَها وَنِساءَ المَمْلَكَةِ يَوْمًا بَعْدَ يَوْمٍ، بَيْنَما كانَتْ تَقودُ المَلِكَ شَهْرَيار نَحْوَ الفَهْمِ وَالتَّغَيُّرِ الحَقيقِيِّ.

Questions

1. لِماذا ظَهَرَ الجِنِّيُّ لِلتَّاجِرِ وَهَدَّدَ بِقَتْلِهِ؟

2. ما الشَّرْطُ الَّذي وَضَعَهُ الجِنِّيُّ لِلتَّاجِرِ قَبْلَ أَنْ يَقْتُلَهُ؟

3. مِنْ هُمُ الأَشْخاصُ الَّذينَ التَقى بِهِمُ التَّاجِرُ أَثْناءَ رِحْلَتِهِ لِمُواجَهَةِ الجِنِّيِّ؟

4. كَيْفَ اسْتَطاعَ العَجوزُ أَنْ يُقْنِعَ الجِنِّيَّ بِعَدَمِ قَتْلِ التَّاجِرِ؟

5. ما العِبْرَةُ الَّتي تَعَلَّمَها التّاجِرُ مِنْ هَذِهِ التَّجْرِبَةِ؟

Answers

1. ظَهَرَ الجِنِّيُّ للتّاجِرِ وَهَدَّدَ بِقَتْلِهِ لِأَنَّ التّاجِرَ قَطَعَ غُصْنَ الشَّجَرَةِ الَّتي كانَتْ مَأْوًى لِلْجِنِّيِّ.

2. الشَّرْطُ الَّذي وَضَعَهُ الجِنِّيُّ هُوَ السَّماحُ لِلتّاجِرِ بِالْعَوْدَةِ إلى عائِلَتِهِ لِمُدَّةِ عامٍ واحِدٍ لِيُوَدِّعَهُمْ وَيَدْفَعَ دُيونَهُ، وَلَكِنْ يَجِبُ أَنْ يَعودَ بَعْدَ مُرورِ العامِ لِيُقْتَلَ.

3. اِلْتَقى التّاجِرُ بِرَجُلٍ عَجوزٍ يَحْمِلُ عَصًا طَويلَةً، وَرَجُلٍ يَحْمِلُ جَرَّةَ ماءٍ، وَآخَرَ يُمْسِكُ حَبْلًا طَويلًا.

4. اِسْتَطاعَ العَجوزُ أَنْ يُقْنِعَ الجِنِّيَّ بِعَدَمِ قَتْلِ التّاجِرِ بِإِظْهارِ قيمَةِ الحَياةِ وَكَيْفَ يُمْكِنُ اسْتِخْدامُ الأَدَواتِ المُخْتَلِفَةِ لِلْعَيْشِ بِسَلامٍ وَتَعاوُنٍ.

5. تَعَلَّمَ التّاجِرُ مِنْ هَذِهِ التَّجْرِبَةِ قيمَةَ التَّعاوُنِ والصَّداقَةِ وَأَنَّ الحَياةَ تَحْمِلُ الكَثيرَ مِنَ العِبَرِ والحِكْمَةِ.

Chapter 2: The Tale of the Merchant and the Genie

On the second night of Scheherazade's stories, she began narrating a tale about a wealthy merchant and a powerful genie. One day, the merchant decided to travel to a faraway city to sell his goods. Before starting his journey, he stopped at a peaceful forest to rest and have his meal.

In the forest, the merchant cut a branch of a tree to light a fire and warm his food. Suddenly, a furious and powerful genie appeared before the merchant and yelled, "Oh human, you have cut the branch of the tree that was my shelter, and for that, I will kill you!"

The merchant was frightened and panicked, and he began pleading with the genie to forgive him and spare his life. He told the genie that he had a family and friends who relied on him, and they would die of grief if they lost him. The genie listened to the merchant and decided to give him a chance to make amends for his mistake.

The genie promised the merchant that he would allow him to return to his family for a period of one year to say goodbye to them and pay off his debts, but on the condition that he would return after the year had passed for the genie to kill him. The merchant agreed to the condition and returned to his city with a heavy heart filled with sadness and fear.

At the end of the year, the merchant started his journey back to the forest to face his inevitable fate. On the way, he met an old man carrying a long stick. The merchant narrated his story to the old man about the genie and the promise he made. The old man showed sympathy to the merchant and decided to accompany him to the forest.

As they continued their journey, the merchant and the old man met two other men: one carrying a jug of water and the other holding a long rope. The two men joined the merchant and the old man, and they all headed toward the forest to confront the genie.

When they reached the forest, the genie appeared and threatened to kill the merchant. The old man intervened and asked the genie if he would allow him to ask three questions before he killed the merchant. The genie agreed to the old man's request.

The old man asked the first question about himself, "How did the long stick benefit me?" and he answered that he used it to measure the depth of the river before crossing it to ensure his safety. Then the old man asked the second question, "What is the benefit of the jug?" and the man carrying the jug replied that he used it to store water and could use it to extinguish a fire in case of an emergency. Finally, the old man asked the third question, "Why are you carrying the long rope?" and the third man replied that he used the rope to climb mountains and could use it to save people stranded on its peaks.

Based on the answers of the three questions, the old man told the genie, "The three of us used these tools for help and survival, and this teaches us that life is valuable, and we must use what is in our hands to live in peace and cooperation. Didn't you consider that, O genie?" The genie was moved by the old man's words and decided to spare the merchant and forgive him.

After this terrifying and difficult experience, the merchant returned to his city and thanked the three men for their help and sacrifice. Despite his fear and the tension he went through, the merchant learned the value of cooperation and friendship and that life carries many lessons and wisdom.

Meanwhile, King Shahryar listened passionately to the story of Scheherazade. He began to develop an attachment to the characters of the story and sympathize with their feelings and struggles. Thanks to this story, the king began to see life through new eyes and realized that people could change and that wisdom and lessons come from different experiences.

On the following night, Scheherazade finished telling the story of the merchant and the genie and began to narrate a new story. In this way, Scheherazade continued to establish trust between her and King Shahryar and taught him valuable lessons about love, humanity, and justice through wonderful stories full of wisdom.

With each story told by Scheherazade, Dinarzad was always by her side, playing her role in making the king interested and eager to hear more. Thus, Scheherazade saved herself and the women of the kingdom day by day while leading King Shahryar toward true understanding and change.

Questions

1. Why did the genie appear to the merchant and threaten to kill him?
2. What was the condition that the genie set for the merchant before killing him?
3. Who were the people that the merchant met on his journey to confront the genie?
4. How did the old man manage to convince the genie not to kill the merchant?
5. What lesson did the merchant learn from this experience?

Answers

1. The genie appeared to the merchant and threatened to kill him because the merchant cut a branch from the tree, which was the genie's shelter.
2. The condition that the genie set for the merchant before killing him was to allow him to return to his

family for one year to say goodbye to them and collect his debts, but he must return after the year to be killed.

3. The merchant met an old man carrying a long stick, a man carrying a jar of water, and another holding a long rope.

4. The old man managed to convince the genie not to kill the merchant by showing the value of life and how different tools can be used to live in peace and cooperation.

5. The merchant learned from this experience the value of cooperation and friendship and that life holds many lessons and wisdom.

الفَصْلُ الثَّالِثُ
الصَّيَّادُ وَالسَّمَكَةُ الذَّهَبِيَّةُ

في إِحْدى المَمالِكِ البَعيدَةِ، كانَ هُناكَ صَيّادٌ فَقيرٌ يَعيشُ مَعَ زَوْجَتِهِ في كوخٍ صَغيرٍ بِجانِبِ البَحْرِ. كانَ يَعْتَمِدُ عَلى الصَّيْدِ لِإِعالَةِ عائِلَتِهِ الصَّغيرَةِ. في أَحَدِ الأَيّامِ، أَلْقى الصَّيّادُ شَبَكَتَهُ في البَحْرِ بَحْثًا عَنْ سَمَكٍ لِبَيْعِهِ في السّوقِ. بَعْدَ ساعاتٍ طَويلَةٍ مِنَ الاِنْتِظارِ، اِنْتَشَلَ الشَّبَكَةَ وَوَجَدَ سَمَكَةً ذَهَبِيَّةً صَغيرَةً عالِقَةً بَيْنَ الحِبالِ.

فوجِئَ الصَّيَّادُ بِهذا الاكْتِشافِ، وَتأمَّلَ السَّمَكَةَ الذَّهَبِيَّةَ الَّتي كانَتْ تَلْمَعُ بِألْوانٍ زاهِيَةٍ تَحْتَ أشِعَّةِ الشَّمْسِ. فَجْأةً، بَدَأتِ السَّمَكَةُ تَتَحَدَّثُ بِصَوْتٍ واضِحٍ، وَطَلَبَتْ مِنَ الصَّيَّادِ أنْ يَتْرُكَها تَحْيا مُقابِلَ تَحْقيقِ ثَلاثِ أُمْنِيّاتٍ لَهُ.

فَكَّرَ الصَّيَّادُ في هذا العَرْضِ المُغْري، وَبَعْدَ تَرَدُّدٍ قَرَّرَ أنْ يُوافِقَ على طَلَبِ السَّمَكَةِ الذَّهَبِيَّةِ. وَعِنْدَما أطْلَقَ سَراحَها، طَلَبَ الصَّيَّادُ أُمْنِيَّتَهُ الأولى: مَنْزِلٌ جَديدٌ وَمُريحٌ لِعائِلَتِهِ. فَظَهَرَ مَنْزِلٌ فاخِرٌ بِجِوارِ الكوخِ القَديمِ على الفَوْرِ.

لَمْ يُصَدِّقِ الصَّيَّادُ وَزَوْجَتُهُ حَظَّهُما السَّعيدَ، وَشَكَرا السَّمَكَةَ الذَّهَبِيَّةَ وَعاشا حَياةً مُرَفَّهَةً في مَنْزِلِهِما الجَديدِ. بَعْدَ مُرورِ بَعْضِ الوَقْتِ، أرادَ الصَّيَّادُ أنْ يَتَوَجَّهَ إلى البَحْرِ مَرَّةً أُخْرى لِطَلَبِ أُمْنِيَّتِهِ الثّانِيَةِ: أنْ يُصْبِحَ غَنِيًّا وَيَتَمَتَّعَ بِثَرْوَةٍ هائِلَةٍ. وَفي اللَّحْظَةِ الَّتي تَمَنَّى فيها ذَلِكَ، امْتَلَأَ مَنْزِلُهُ بِالذَّهَبِ وَالجَواهِرِ.

بِهَذِهِ الثَّرْوَةِ الهائِلَةِ، أصْبَحَ الصَّيَّادُ وَزَوْجَتُهُ مِنْ أغْنى النّاسِ في

المَمْلَكَةِ. اِشْتَرَوْا مَلابِسَ فاخِرَةً وَأَقامُوا مَآدِبَ عَشاءٍ لِأَصْدِقائِهِمْ وَجيرانِهِمْ، وَعاشُوا حَياةَ النُّبَلاءِ. وَمَعَ ذَلِكَ، بَدَأَ الصَّيادُ يَشْعُرُ بِالْفَراغِ وَالرَّغْبَةِ في المَزيدِ، فَقَرَّرَ طَلَبَ أُمْنِيَّتِهِ الثّالِثَةِ مِنَ السَّمَكَةِ الذَّهَبِيَّةِ.

ذَهَبَ الصَّيادُ إِلى الشاطِئِ وَنادى السَّمَكَةَ الذَّهَبِيَّةَ الَّتي خَرَجَتْ مِنَ الماءِ واسْتَمَعَتْ لِطَلَبِهِ. قالَ الصَّيادُ: "أَرْغَبُ في أَنْ أُصْبِحَ مَلِكًا عَلى هَذِهِ المَمْلَكَةِ وَأَحْكُمَها بِعَدْلٍ وَرَحْمَةٍ." وافَقَتِ السَّمَكَةُ الذَّهَبِيَّةُ عَلى طَلَبِهِ وَتَحَقَّقَتْ أُمْنِيَّتُهُ عَلى الفَوْرِ.

أَصْبَحَ الصَّيادُ مَلِكًا عَظيمًا وَعاشَ في قَصْرٍ رائِعٍ مَعَ زَوْجَتِهِ وَأُمَرائِهِ. حَكَمَ بِعَدْلٍ وَرَحْمَةٍ وَسَعى لِتَحْسينِ حَياةِ شَعْبِهِ. لَكِنْ مَعَ مُرورِ الوَقْتِ، بَدَأَ يُعاني مِنَ القَلَقِ وَالضُّغوطِ المُتَزايِدَةِ الَّتي تَأْتي مَعَ الحُكْمِ، وَشَعَرَ بِالتَّعَبِ وَالغَضَبِ مِنَ التَّحَدِّياتِ اليَوْمِيَّةِ.

في لَيْلَةٍ هادِئَةٍ، تَأَمَّلَ المَلِكُ الصَّيادُ حَياتَهُ وَتَذَكَّرَ الأَيّامَ البَسيطَةَ عِنْدَما كانَ يَصْطادُ سَمَكًا وَيَعيشُ بِسَلامٍ مَعَ زَوْجَتِهِ. تَأَلَّمَ قَلْبُهُ لِفُقْدانِ تِلْكَ الأَيّامِ، وَقَرَّرَ أَنْ يَطْلُبَ مُساعَدَةَ السَّمَكَةِ الذَّهَبِيَّةِ مَرَّةً

أُخْرى.

ذَهَبَ المَلِكُ إِلى الشَّاطِئِ وَنادى السَّمَكَةَ الذَّهَبِيَّةِ، الَّتي خَرَجَتْ مِنَ الماءِ. طَلَبَ مِنْها أَنْ تُعيدَهُ إِلى حَياتِهِ البَسيطَةِ كَصَيَّادٍ فَقيرٍ، وَأَنْ تَأْخُذَ مَعَها كُلَّ الثَّرَواتِ وَالمُلْكِ. اِبْتَسَمَتِ السَّمَكَةُ الذَّهَبِيَّةُ وَوافَقَتْ عَلى طَلَبِهِ، فَعادَ الصَّيَّادُ وَزَوْجَتُهُ إِلى الكوخِ البَسيطِ عَلى الشَّاطِئِ، وَعاشا حَياةً هادِئَةً وَسَعيدَةً مَليئَةً بِالْمَحَبَّةِ وَالرِّضا.

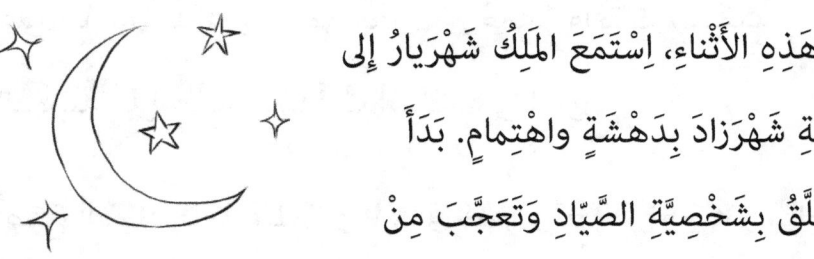

في هَذِهِ الأَثْناءِ، اِسْتَمَعَ المَلِكُ شَهْرَيارُ إِلى قِصَّةِ شَهْرَزادَ بِدَهْشَةٍ واهْتِمامٍ. بَدَأَ يَتَعَلَّقُ بِشَخْصِيَّةِ الصَّيَّادِ وَتَعَجَّبَ مِنْ حِكْمَةِ السَّمَكَةِ الذَّهَبِيَّةِ. بَعْدَ أَنْ أَنْهَتْ شَهْرَزادُ قِصَّتها، أَعْلَنَ المَلِكُ شَهْرَيارُ أَنَّهُ يَرْغَبُ في سَماعِ المَزيدِ مِنَ القِصَصِ وَأَنَّهُ لَنْ يَقْتُلَها في الصَّباحِ التَّالي.

Questions

1. ماذا وَجَدَ الصَّيّادُ في شَبَكَتِهِ عِنْدَما انْتَشَلَها مِنَ البَحْرِ؟

2. ماذا عَرَضَتِ السَّمَكَةُ الذَّهَبِيَّةُ عَلى الصَّيّادِ مُقابِلَ إِطْلاقِ سَراحِها؟

3. ما هِيَ الأُمْنِيَّةُ الثّانِيَةُ الَّتي طَلَبَها الصَّيّادُ مِنَ السَّمَكَةِ الذَّهَبِيَّةِ؟

4. كَيْفَ شَعَرَ المَلِكُ الصَّيّادُ بَعْدَ أَنْ أَصْبَحَ مَلِكًا عَلى المَمْلَكَةِ؟

5. ما هُوَ الطَّلَبُ الأخيرُ الَّذي طَلَبَهُ المَلِكُ الصَّيّادُ مِنَ السَّمَكَةِ الذَّهَبِيَّةِ؟

Answers

1. وَجَدَ الصَّيّادُ سَمَكَةً ذَهَبِيَّةً صَغيرَةً عالِقَةً بَيْنَ الحِبالِ.

2. عَرَضَتِ السَّمَكَةُ الذَّهَبِيَّةُ تَحْقيقَ ثَلاثِ أُمْنِيّاتٍ لِلصَّيّادِ مُقابِلَ أَنْ يَتْرُكَها تَحْيا.

3. طَلَبَ الصَّيّادُ أَنْ يُصْبِحَ غَنِيًّا وَيَتَمَتَّعَ بِثَرْوَةٍ هائِلَةٍ.

4. شَعَرَ المَلِكُ الصَّيّادُ بِالْقَلَقِ وَالضُّغوطِ المُتَزايِدَةِ الَّتي تَأْتي مَعَ الحُكْمِ، وَالتَّعَبِ وَالغَضَبِ مِنَ التَّحَدِّياتِ اليَوْمِيَّةِ.

5. طَلَبَ المَلِكُ الصَّيّادُ أَنْ يَعودَ إِلى حَياتِهِ البَسيطَةِ كَصَيّادٍ فَقيرٍ وَأَنْ تَأْخُذَ السَّمَكَةُ الذَّهَبِيَّةُ كُلَّ الثَّرَواتِ وَالمُلْكِ.

Chapter 3: The Fisherman and the Golden Fish

In a distant kingdom, there was a poor fisherman who lived with his wife in a small hut by the sea. He relied on fishing to support his small family. One day, the fisherman cast his net into the sea in search of fish to sell in the market. After hours of waiting, he pulled up his net and found a small golden fish trapped among the ropes.

The fisherman was surprised by this discovery and marveled at the golden fish that shimmered in bright colors under the sunlight. Suddenly, the fish began to speak in a clear voice and asked the fisherman to spare its life in exchange for granting him three wishes.

The fisherman thought about this tempting offer and, after some hesitation, decided to agree to the golden fish's request. And when he released it, the fisherman made his first wish: a new and comfortable home for his family. A luxurious house appeared next to the old hut immediately.

The fisherman and his wife could not believe their good luck and thanked the golden fish. They lived a luxurious life in their new home. After some time, the fisherman wanted to go to the sea again to make his second wish: to become rich and have immense wealth. And at the moment he wished for it, his house was filled with gold and jewels.

With this immense wealth, the fisherman and his wife became some of the richest people in the kingdom. They bought luxurious clothes and held dinner parties for their friends and neighbors, and lived the life of nobles. However, the fisherman began to feel empty and wanted more, so he decided to make his third wish to the golden fish.

The fisherman went to the beach and called out to the golden fish that emerged from the water and listened to his request. The fisherman said, "I want to become the king of this kingdom and rule it with justice and mercy." The golden fish agreed to his request, and his wish was immediately granted.

The fisherman became a great king and lived in a magnificent palace with his wife and princes. He ruled with justice and mercy and sought to improve the lives of his people. But over time, he began to suffer from the increasing pressure and anxiety that comes with ruling, and felt tired and angry from the daily challenges.

On a quiet night, the fisherman king reflected on his life and remembered the simple days when he used to fish and live in peace with his wife. His heart ached for those days, and he decided to seek the help of the golden fish once again.

The king went to the beach and called out to the golden fish that emerged from the water. He asked her to return him to his simple life as a poor fisherman and to take all of his wealth and possessions with it. The golden fish smiled and granted his request, so the fisherman and his wife returned to their simple hut on the beach and lived a quiet and happy life filled with love and contentment.

Meanwhile, King Shahryar listened to Scheherazade's story with amazement and interest. He began to relate to the fisherman's character and admired the wisdom of the golden fish. After Scheherazade finished her story, King Shahryar announced that he wanted to hear more stories and that he would not kill her the next morning.

Questions

1. What did the fisherman find in his net when he pulled it out of the sea?
2. What did the golden fish offer the fisherman in exchange for its release?
3. What was the second wish that the fisherman asked the golden fish to grant him?
4. How did the king fisherman feel after becoming the ruler of the kingdom?
5. What was the last request that king the fisherman made to the golden fish?

Answers

1. The fisherman found a small golden fish trapped in the ropes.

2. The golden fish offered to grant three wishes to the fisherman in exchange for sparing its life.

3. The fisherman asked to become rich and enjoy immense wealth.

4. The king fisherman felt anxious and overwhelmed with the pressures that come with ruling, tired and angry with the daily challenges.

5. King fisherman asked to return to his simple life as a poor fisherman and for the golden fish to take all the wealth and the kingdom.

الفَصْلُ الرّابِعُ
عَلاءُ الدّينِ وَالْمِصْباحُ السِّحْريُّ

فِي اللَّيْلَةِ التّالِيَةِ، بَدَأَتْ شَهْرَزادُ تَرْوِي قِصَّةً مُفَصَّلَةً وَمُشَوِّقَةً عَنْ عَلاءِ الدّينِ وَالْمِصْباحِ السِّحْرِيِّ لِلْمَلِكِ شَهْرَيارَ.

كانَ عَلاءُ الدّينِ شابًّا فَقيرًا يَعيشُ مَعَ والِدَتِهِ الأَرْمَلَةِ فِي أَحَدِ أَحْياءِ المَدينَةِ. كانَ يَعْمَلُ فِي النَّهارِ وَيَجوبُ الأَسْواقَ وَالشَّوارِعَ، بَيْنَما

كانَتْ والِدَتُهُ تقومُ بِالأعْمالِ المَنْزِلِيَّةِ.

ذاتَ يَوْمٍ، وَبَيْنَما كانَ عَلاءُ الدّينِ يَتَجَوَّلُ في السّوقِ، الْتَقى بِرَجُلٍ غَريبٍ زَعَمَ أنَّهُ عَمُّهُ الّذي طالَما سَمِعَ عَلاءُ الدّينِ عَنْهُ مِنْ والِدَتِهِ. ادَّعى الرَّجُلُ الغَريبُ أنَّهُ جاءَ لِزِيارَةِ عائلَتِهِ، وَأنَّهُ يَعْرِفُ مَكانًا سِرِّيًّا فيهِ كَنْزٌ عَظيمٌ مَخْفِيٌّ. قَدْ يَكونُ هَذا الكَنْزُ مِفْتاحَ الثَّراءِ وَالنَّجاحِ لِعَلاءِ الدّينِ وَوالِدَتِهِ. عَلى الرَّغْمِ مِنْ شُكوكِهِ، قَرَّرَ عَلاءُ الدّينِ الانْضِمامَ إلى الرَّجُلِ الغَريبِ في رِحْلَةِ البَحْثِ عَنِ الكَنْزِ.

قادَهُ الرَّجُلُ الغَريبُ إلى مَغارَةٍ مُظْلِمَةٍ وَسِرِّيَّةٍ في أعْماقِ الصَّحْراءِ. طَلَبَ مِنْ عَلاءِ الدّينِ أنْ يَدْخُلَ المَغارَةَ وَيَجْلِبَ المِصْباحَ القَديمَ المَوْجودَ هُناكَ، مُشيرًا إلى أنَّ هَذا المِصْباحَ يَمْتَلِكُ قُوَّةً سِحْرِيَّةً لا يُمْكِنُ تَصَوُّرُها. تَسَلَّلَ عَلاءُ الدّينِ إلى المَغارَةِ وَعَثَرَ عَلى المِصْباحِ السِّحْرِيِّ. وَمَعَ ذَلِكَ، بِمُجَرَّدِ أنْ أمْسَكَ بِهِ، أغْلَقَ الرَّجُلُ الغَريبُ مَدْخَلَ المَغارَةِ وَتَرَكَ عَلاءَ الدّينِ مُحْتَجَزًا داخِلَها، كانَ قَدْ خَطَّطَ لِسَرِقَةِ المِصْباحِ مِنْهُ لاحِقًا.

في مُحاوَلَةٍ لِلخُروجِ مِنَ المَغارَةِ، بَدَأَ عَلاءُ الدّينِ يَبْحَثُ عَنْ طَريقٍ لِلخُروجِ. وَجَدَ المِصْباحَ القَديمَ وَرَأى أَنَّهُ قَدْ يَكونُ مُفيدًا لِإضاءَةِ المَغارَةِ المُظْلِمَةِ وَالبَحْثِ عَنِ المَخْرَجِ. بَدَأَ يَفْرُكُ المِصْباحَ السِّحْرِيَّ، وَفَجْأَةً ظَهَرَ جِنِّيٌّ عِمْلاقٌ. قالَ لَهُ الجِنِّيُّ: "أَنا جِنِّيُّ المِصْباحِ السِّحْرِيِّ، وَأَنا هُنا لِتَحْقيقِ ثَلاثِ أُمْنِيّاتٍ تَطْلُبُها." لَمْ يَسْتَوْعِبْ عَلاءُ الدّينِ تَمامًا ما حَدَثَ، لَكِنَّهُ قَرَّرَ اسْتِغْلالَ الفُرْصَةِ لِلهُروبِ مِنَ المَغارَةِ. طَلَبَ مِنَ الجِنِّيِّ أَنْ يَنْقُلَهُ إِلى بَيْتِهِ في المَدينَةِ، وَفي لَمْحِ البَصَرِ وَجَدَ عَلاءُ الدّينِ نَفْسَهُ بِجِوارِ والِدَتِهِ الَّتي كانَتْ قَلِقَةً عَلى ابْنِها وَلَمْ تَعْرِفْ مَصيرَهُ. أَخْبَرَ عَلاءُ الدّينِ والِدَتَهُ بِما حَدَثَ وَعَنِ الجِنِّيِّ وَالمِصْباحِ السِّحْرِيِّ. بَدَآ يُدْرِكانِ مَدى قُوَّةِ المِصْباحِ وَكَيْفَ يُمْكِنُ اسْتِخْدامُهُ لِتَحْسينِ حَياتِهِما.

طَلَبَ عَلاءُ الدّينِ مِنَ الجِنِّيِّ أَنْ يَجْلِبَ لَهُما ثَرْوَةً هائِلَةً تَسْمَحُ لَهُما بِالعَيْشِ بِرَفاهِيَةٍ. وَبِفَضْلِ هَذِهِ الثَّرْوَةِ، تَغَيَّرَتْ حَياةُ عَلاءِ الدّينِ وَوالِدَتِهِ تَمامًا. اِشْتَرَيا قَصْرًا جَميلًا وَأَصْبَحَ عَلاءُ الدّينِ شَخْصِيَّةً مُهِمَّةً في المَدينَةِ. وَمَعَ مُرورِ الوَقْتِ، أَدْرَكَ عَلاءُ الدّينِ أَنَّهُ يَرْغَبُ في الزَّواجِ مِنَ الأَميرَةِ الجَميلَةِ، ابْنَةِ السُّلْطانِ. اِسْتَخْدَمَ

المِصْباحَ السِّحْرِيَّ لِيُساعِدَهُ على كَسْبِ قَلْبِ الأَميرَةِ وَيَسْمَحَ لَهُ بِالزَّواجِ مِنها.

في تِلْكَ الأَثْناءِ، عادَ الرَّجُلُ الغَريبُ لِيَسْتَعيدَ المِصْباحَ السِّحْرِيَّ الَّذي ظَنَّ أَنَّهُ سُرِقَ مِنْهُ. خَطَّطَ لِسَرِقَتِهِ مِنْ عَلاءِ الدّينِ واسْتِخْدامِ قُوَّتِهِ لِلسَّيْطَرَةِ عَلَى المَدينَةِ وَفَرْضِ هَيْمَنَتِهِ عَلى سُكّانِها. وَلَكِنَّ عَلاءَ الدّينِ وَالأَميرَةَ تَعاوَنا مَعًا لِلتَّصَدّي لِلْخَطَرِ الَّذي يُهَدِّدُ حَياتَهُما وَمُسْتَقْبَلَ المَدينَةِ.

في المَعْرَكَةِ النِّهائِيَّةِ، تَمَكَّنَ عَلاءُ الدّينِ وَالأَميرَةُ مِنَ اسْتِعادَةِ المِصْباحِ السِّحْرِيِّ مِنَ الرَّجُلِ الغَريبِ وَهَزيمَتِهِ. اِحْتَفَظَ عَلاءُ الدّينِ بِالمِصْباحِ، لَكِنَّهُ تَعَهَّدَ بِعَدَمِ الاِعْتِمادِ عَلَيْهِ في المُسْتَقْبَلِ إِلّا في حالاتِ الضَّرورَةِ القُصْوى. تَزَوَّجَ عَلاءُ الدّينِ وَالأَميرَةُ وَعاشا مَعًا في سَعادَةٍ دائِمَةٍ.

اِنْتَهَتْ شَهْرَزادُ مِنْ سَرْدِ قِصَّةِ عَلاءِ الدّينِ وَالمِصْباحِ السِّحْرِيِّ. كانَ المَلِكُ شَهْرَيارُ مَفْتونًا بِهَذِهِ القِصَّةِ وَمُتَشَوِّقًا لِسَماعِ

المَزيدِ مِنَ القِصَصِ المُلْهِمَةِ وَالمُثيرَةِ. أَدْرَكَ المَلِكُ شَهْرَيارُ أَنَّ كُلَّ قِصَّةٍ تَحْمِلُ في طَيَّاتِها دُروسًا هامَّةً عَنِ الحَياةِ وَالحِكْمَةِ وَالعَدْلِ.

Questions

1. ما هِيَ الطَّريقَةُ الَّتي التَقى بِها عَلاءُ الدّينِ بِالرَّجُلِ الغَريبِ؟

2. ماذا طَلَبَ الرَّجُلُ الغَريبُ مِنْ عَلاءِ الدّينِ عِنْدَما أَخَذَهُ إلى المَغارَةِ؟

3. كَيْفَ تَمَكَّنَ عَلاءُ الدّينِ مِنَ الهُروبِ مِنَ المَغارَةِ؟

4. كَيْفَ اسْتَخْدَمَ عَلاءُ الدّينِ المِصْباحَ السِّحْرِيَّ لِتَحْسينِ حَياتِهِ وَحَياةِ والِدَتِهِ؟

5. ما هُوَ الخَطَرُ الَّذي واجَهَهُ عَلاءُ الدّينِ وَالأَميرَةُ؟

Answers

1. اِلتَقى عَلاءُ الدّينِ بِالرَّجُلِ الغَريبِ عِنْدَما كانَ يَتَجَوَّلُ في السّوقِ.

2. طَلَبَ مِنْ عَلاءِ الدّينِ أَنْ يَدْخُلَ المَغارَةَ وَيَجْلِبَ المِصْباحَ القَديمَ المَوْجودَ هُناكَ.

3. تَمَكَّنَ عَلاءُ الدّينِ مِنَ الهُروبِ مِنَ المَغارَةِ عَنْ طَريقِ طَلَبِ المُساعَدَةِ مِنَ الجِنّيِّ الَّذي خَرَجَ عِنْدَما فَرَكَ المِصْباحَ السِّحْرِيَّ.

4. طَلَبَ عَلاءُ الدّينِ مِنَ الجِنّيِّ أَنْ يَجْلِبَ لَهُما ثَرْوَةً هائِلَةً، مِمّا سَمَحَ لَهُما بِشِراءِ قَصْرٍ جَميلٍ وَتَغْييرِ حَياتِهِما تَمامًا.

5. عادَ الرَّجُلُ الغَريبُ لِيَسْتَعيدَ المِصْباحَ السِّحْرِيَّ وَيَسْتَخْدِمَ قُوَّتَهُ لِلسَّيْطَرَةِ عَلى المَدينَةِ، لَكِنَّ عَلاءَ الدّينِ وَالأَميرَةَ تَصَدَّيا لَهُ وَهَزَماهُ في المَعْرَكَةِ النِّهائِيَّةِ.

Chapter 4: Aladdin and the Magic Lamp

On the following night, Scheherazade began to tell an intricate and captivating story about Aladdin and the Magic Lamp to King Shahryar.

Aladdin was a poor young man who lived with his widowed mother in one of the city's neighborhoods. He worked during the day, wandering through the markets and streets, while his mother did household chores.

One day, while Aladdin was strolling through the market, he met a strange man who claimed to be his long-lost uncle, whom Aladdin had only heard about from his mother. The stranger claimed that he had come to visit his family and that he knew of a secret place where a great treasure was hidden. This treasure could be the key to Aladdin's and his mother's wealth and success. Despite his suspicions, Aladdin decided to join the strange man on a quest to find the treasure.

The man led him to a dark and secret cave in the depths of the desert. He asked Aladdin to enter the cave and retrieve the old lamp that was there, indicating that this lamp possessed an unimaginable magical power. Aladdin sneaked into the cave and found the magic lamp. However, once he held it, the stranger closed the cave's entrance and left Aladdin trapped inside, planning to steal the lamp from him later.

In an attempt to get out of the cave, Aladdin started looking for a way out. He found the old lamp and thought it might be useful to light up the dark cave and to search for the exit. He began to rub the magic lamp, and suddenly a giant genie appeared. The genie told him, "I am the genie of the magic lamp, and I am here to grant three wishes that you asked for." Aladdin did not fully comprehend what was happening, but he decided to seize the opportunity to escape from the cave. He asked the genie to transport him to his home in the city, and in the blink of an eye, Aladdin found himself next to his mother, who had been worried about her son's fate. Aladdin told his mother what had happened and about the genie and the magic lamp. They both began to realize the lamp's power and how it could be used to improve their lives.

Aladdin asked the genie to bring them immense wealth that would allow them to live in luxury. Thanks to this wealth, Aladdin's and his mother's lives changed completely. They bought a beautiful palace, and Aladdin became an important figure in the city. As time passed, Aladdin realized that he wanted to marry the beautiful princess, the sultan's daughter. He used the magic lamp to help him win the princess's heart and allow him to marry her.

In the meantime, the strange man returned to reclaim the magic lamp that he felt was stolen from him. He planned to steal it from Aladdin and use its power to control the city and impose his dominance over its inhabitants. But Aladdin and the princess cooperated to confront the danger threatening their lives and the future of the city.

In the final battle, Aladdin and the princess managed to retrieve the magic lamp from the strange man and defeat him. Aladdin kept the lamp but pledged not to rely on it in the future except in cases of extreme necessity. Aladdin and the princess got married and lived happily ever after.

Scheherazade finished telling the story of Aladdin and the magic lamp to King Shahriyar. The king was fascinated by this story and eager to hear more inspiring and exciting tales. King Shahriyar realized that every story carries important lessons about life, wisdom, and justice.

Questions

1. How did Aladdin meet the mysterious man?
2. What did the mysterious man ask Aladdin to do when he took him to the cave?
3. How did Aladdin escape from the cave?
4. How did Aladdin use the magic lamp to improve his and his mother's life?
5. What danger did Aladdin and the princess face?

Answers

1. Aladdin met the mysterious man when he was wandering in the market.

2. The mysterious man asked Aladdin to enter the cave and bring the old lamp that was there.

3. Aladdin managed to escape from the cave by requesting help from the genie who came out when he rubbed the magic lamp.

4. Aladdin asked the genie to bring them immense wealth, which allowed them to buy a beautiful palace and completely change their lives.

5. The mysterious man returned to retrieve the magic lamp and use its power to control the city, but Aladdin and the princess confronted him and defeated him in the final battle.

الفَصلُ الخامِسُ
عَلي بابا وَالأَربَعونَ لِصًّا

عِندَما انتَهَتْ شَهْرَزادُ مِنْ قِصَّةِ عَلاءِ الدّينِ وَالمِصباحِ السِّحريِّ، كانَ المَلِكُ شَهْرَيارُ مُتَحَمِّسًا لِسَماعِ المَزيدِ مِنَ القِصَصِ العَجيبَةِ وَالمَليئَةِ بِالمُغامَراتِ. وَفي تِلكَ اللَّيْلَةِ، بَدَأَتْ شَهْرَزادُ تَروي قِصَّةَ عَلي بابا وَالأَربَعينَ لِصًّا.

كانَ عَلي بابا رَجُلًا بَسيطًا وَفقيرًا يَعيشُ في قَرْيَةٍ نائِيَةٍ مَعَ زَوْجَتِهِ وابْنِهِ. وَفي أَحَدِ الأَيّامِ، كانَ عَلي بابا يَجْمَعُ الحَطَبَ في الغابَةِ حينَ سَمِعَ صَوْتَ حَوافِرَ عَلى الأَرْضِ وَضَجيجَ رِجالٍ يَتَكَلَّمونَ بِصَوْتٍ عالٍ. رَأى رَجُلًا يَبْدو أَنَّهُ رَئيسُ عِصابَةٍ مِنْ أَرْبَعينَ لِصًّا، وَعِنْدَما اقْتَرَبوا مِنْ صَخْرَةٍ ضَخْمَةٍ، قالَ القائِدُ كَلِمَةً سِرِّيَّةً: "اِفْتَحْ يا سِمْسِمْ!" فانْفَتَحَتِ الصَّخْرَةُ كاشِفَةً عَنْ مَدْخَلٍ سِرِّيٍّ إِلى كَهْفٍ ضَخْمٍ مَليءٍ بِالكُنوزِ وَالذَّهَبِ.

بَعْدَ مُغادَرَةِ اللُّصوصِ الكَهْفَ، تَوَجَّهَ عَلي بابا نَحْوَ الصَّخْرَةِ العِمْلاقَةِ واسْتَخْدَمَ الكَلِمَةَ السِّرِّيَّةَ لِفَتْحِ المَدْخَلِ. وَعِنْدَما دَخَلَ الكَهْفَ، فوجِئَ بِالكُنوزِ الهائِلَةِ الَّتي يَمْتَلِكُها الأَرْبَعونَ لِصًّا. قَرَّرَ عَلي بابا أَنْ يَأْخُذَ بَعْضَ الذَّهَبِ وَيَعودَ بِهِ إِلى مَنْزِلِهِ.

بَعْدَ عَوْدَتِهِ لِلْمَنْزِلِ، شَرَحَ عَلي بابا لِزَوْجَتِهِ ما حَدَثَ وَأَخْبَرَها بِالكَنْزِ الَّذي اكْتَشَفَهُ. قاما بِإِخْفاءِ الذَّهَبِ وَقَرَّرا أَنْ يَسْتَخْدِماهُ بِحَذَرٍ لِتَحْسينِ حَياتِهِما. لَكِنْ كانَ لَدى عَلي بابا أَخٌ طَمّاعٌ يُدْعى قاسِمًا، وَعِنْدَما اكْتَشَفَ ما حَدَثَ، أَرادَ أَنْ يَأْخُذَ جُزْءًا مِنَ الكَنْزِ

لِنَفْسِهِ.

ذَهَبَ قاسِمٌ إلى الكَهْفِ واسْتَخْدَمَ الكَلِمَةَ السِّرِّيَّةَ لِفَتْحِ المَدْخَلِ. عِنْدَما دَخَلَ الكَهْفَ، لَمْ يَسْتَطِعِ التَّحَكُّمَ في جَشَعِهِ، وَجَمَعَ كَمِّيَّةً ضَخْمَةً مِنَ الذَّهَبِ والكُنوزِ. لَكِنْ عِنْدَما حاوَلَ الخُروجَ، نَسِيَ الكَلِمَةَ السِّرِّيَّةَ وَعَلِقَ داخِلَ الكَهْفِ.

بَيْنَما كانَ قاسِمٌ مُحاصَرًا داخِلَ الكَهْفِ، عادَ الأَرْبَعونَ لِصًّا وَعَثَروا عَلَيْهِ. عاقَبوهُ بِشِدَّةٍ وَقَتَلوهُ بِسَبَبِ مُحاوَلَتِهِ سَرِقَةَ كَنْزِهِم. عِنْدَما عَلِمَ عَلي بابا بِمَصيرِ شَقيقِهِ، شَعَرَ بِالحُزْنِ والخَوْفِ. قَرَّرَ أَنْ يَتَّخِذَ إِجْراءاتٍ لِحِمايَةِ عائِلَتِهِ مِنَ الأَرْبَعينَ لِصًّا الَّذينَ سَيَسْعَوْنَ لِلْاِنْتِقامِ بِلا شَكٍّ.

في الوَقْتِ نَفْسِهِ، كانَتْ لَدى عَلي بابا خادِمَةٌ ذَكِيَّةٌ وَمُخْلِصَةٌ تُدْعى مَرْجانَةَ. عِنْدَما عَلِمَتْ بِخَطَرِ اللُّصوصِ، قامَتْ بِوَضْعِ خُطَّةٍ لِلتَّخَلُّصِ مِنْهُم. اِسْتَطاعَتْ مَرْجانَةُ، بِمُساعَدَةِ عَلي بابا وابْنِهِ، القَضاءَ عَلى الأَرْبَعينَ لِصًّا والتَّخَلُّصَ مِنْهُم نِهائِيًّا.

بَعْدَ التَّغَلُّبِ عَلى الأَرْبَعينَ لِصًّا، اِسْتَمَرَّ عَلي بابا وَعائِلَتُهُ في

اسْتِخْدامِ الكُنوزِ بِحِكْمَةٍ لِتَحْسينِ حَياتِهِمْ وَمُساعَدَةِ الفُقَراءِ والمُحْتاجينَ في قَرْيَتِهِمْ.

تَزَوَّجَ ابنُ عَلي بابا مَرْجانَةَ تَكْريمًا لِشَجاعَتِها وَذَكائِها، وَعاشُوا جَميعًا حَياةً سَعيدَةً وَمُسْتَقِرَّةً.

اِنْتَهَتْ شَهْرَزادُ مِنْ قِصَّةِ عَلي بابا والأَرْبَعينَ لِصًّا، وَكانَ المَلِكُ شَهْرَيارُ مُتَحَمِّسًا لِسَماعِ قِصَّةٍ جَديدَةٍ وَمُلْهِمَةٍ في اللَّيْلَةِ التّالِيَةِ.

Questions

1. ما هِيَ المِهْنَةُ الَّتي كانَ يُمارِسُها عَلي بابا؟

2. كَيْفَ اكْتَشَفَ عَلي بابا مَكانَ كَنْزِ الأَرْبَعينَ لِصًّا؟

3. ماذا فَعَلَ قاسِمٌ حينَ عَلِمَ بِالْكَنْزِ؟

4. كَيْفَ تُوُفِّيَ قاسِمٌ؟

5. مِنْ هِيَ مَرْجانَةُ وَما دَوْرُها في القِصَّةِ؟

Answers

1. كانَ عَلي بابا رَجُلًا بَسيطًا وَفَقيرًا يَجْمَعُ الحَطَبَ في الغابَةِ.

2. اِكْتَشَفَ عَلي بابا المَكانَ عِنْدَما كانَ يَجْمَعُ الحَطَبَ وَسَمِعَ صَوْتَ حَوافِرَ وَضَجيجَ رِجالٍ يَتَكَلَّمونَ بِصَوْتٍ عالٍ وَرَآهم يَسْتَخْدِمونَ الكَلِمَةَ السِّرِّيَّةَ لِفَتْحِ مَدْخَلِ الكَهْفِ.

3. ذَهَبَ قاسِمٌ إلى الكَهْفِ واستَخْدَمَ الكَلِمَةَ السِّرِّيَّةَ لِفَتْحِ المَدْخَلِ، وَجَمَعَ كَمِّيَّةً ضَخْمَةً مِنَ الذَّهَبِ والكُنوزِ.

4. تُوُفِّيَ قاسِمٌ عِنْدَما عادَ الأَرْبَعونَ لِصًّا وَعَثَروا عَلَيْهِ داخِلَ الكَهْفِ وَقَتَلوهُ بِسَبَبِ مُحاوَلَتِهِ سَرِقَةَ كَنْزِهِمْ.

5. كانَتْ مَرْجانَةُ خادِمَةً عَلي بابا الذَّكِيَّةَ والمُخْلِصَةَ، وَلَعِبَتْ دَوْرًا حاسِمًا في التَّخَلُّصِ مِنَ الأَرْبَعينَ لِصًّا بِمُساعَدَةِ عَلي بابا وابْنِهِ.

Chapter 5: Ali Baba and the Forty Thieves

When Scheherazade finished the story of Aladdin and the Magic Lamp, King Shahryar was excited to hear more amazing stories full of adventures. That night, Scheherazade began to tell the story of Ali Baba and the Forty Thieves.

Ali Baba was a simple and poor man who lived in a remote village with his wife and son. One day, while he was gathering firewood in the forest, he heard the sound of hooves on the ground and the loud voices of men. He saw a man who appeared to be the leader of a group of forty thieves, and when they approached a huge rock, the leader said a secret word: "Open sesame!" and the rock opened to reveal a secret entrance to a huge cave filled with treasures and gold.

After the thieves left the cave, Ali Baba approached the huge rock and used the secret word to open the entrance. When he entered the cave, he was amazed by the enormous treasures that the forty thieves possessed. Ali Baba decided to take some gold and return home with it.

After his return home, Ali Baba explained to his wife what had happened and told her about the treasure he had discovered. They hid the gold and decided to use it cautiously to improve their lives. However, Ali Baba had a greedy brother named Qasim, and when he discovered what had happened, he wanted to take a portion of the treasure for himself.

Qasim went to the cave and used the secret word to open the entrance. When he entered the cave, he could not control his greed and collected a huge amount of gold and treasures. But when he tried to leave, he forgot the secret word and became trapped inside the cave.

While Qasim was trapped inside the cave, the forty thieves returned and found him. They punished him severely and killed him for attempting to steal their treasure. When Ali Baba learned of his brother's fate, he felt sadness and fear. He decided to take measures to protect his family from the forty thieves, who would undoubtedly seek revenge.

At the same time, Ali Baba had a smart and loyal servant named Morgiana. When she learned of the danger posed by the thieves, she devised a plan to get rid of them. With the help of Ali Baba and his son, Morgiana was able to eliminate the forty thieves and get rid of them for good.

After defeating the forty thieves, Ali Baba and his family continued to use the treasure wisely to improve their lives and help the poor and needy in their village. Ali Baba's son married Morgiana in honor of her bravery and intelligence, and they all lived a happy and stable life.

Scheherazade finished telling the story of Ali Baba and the Forty Thieves, and King Shahryar was eager to hear a new and inspiring story the following night.

Questions

1. What was Ali Baba's profession?
2. How did Ali Baba discover the location of the Forty Thieves' treasure?
3. What did Qasim do when he learned about the treasure?
4. How did Qasim die?
5. Who is Morgiana, and what was her role in the story?

Answers

1. Ali Baba was a simple and poor man who collected firewood in the forest.
2. Ali Baba discovered the location when he was collecting firewood and heard the sound of horses' hooves and the noise of men speaking loudly, and saw them using the secret word to open the entrance to the cave.
3. Kasim went to the cave and used the secret word to open the entrance, and collected a huge amount of gold and treasures.
4. Kasim died when the Forty Thieves returned and found him inside the cave, and killed him for attempting to steal their treasure.

5. Morgiana was Ali Baba's smart and loyal servant and played a crucial role in getting rid of the Forty Thieves with the help of Ali Baba and his son.

الفَصْلُ السّادِسُ
الفَلّاحُ الذَّكِيُّ وَالجِنِّيُّ المُشاغِبُ

في اللَّيْلَةِ التّالِيَةِ، بَدَأَتْ شَهْرَزادُ تَروي قِصَّةً جَديدَةً لِلْمَلِكِ شَهْرَيارَ عَنْ فَلّاحٍ ذَكِيٍّ وجِنِّيٍّ مُشاغِبٍ.

كانَ هُناكَ فَلّاحٌ فَقيرٌ يُدْعى يوسُفَ يَعيشُ في قَرْيَةٍ صَغيرَةٍ. كانَ يوسُفُ يَعْمَلُ بِجِدٍّ لِكَسْبِ قوتِ يَوْمِهِ وَإِطْعامِ عائِلَتِهِ. في يَوْمٍ مُشْمِسٍ، قَرَّرَ يوسُفُ أَنْ يَذْهَبَ لِلْحَقْلِ لِقَطْفِ بَعْضِ الفَواكِهِ وَالخَضْراواتِ لِبَيْعِها في السّوقِ. بَيْنَما كانَ يَحْرُثُ الأَرْضَ، اِصْطَدَمَ مِعْوَلُهُ بِجَرَّةٍ غَريبَةٍ مَدْفونَةٍ تَحْتَ الأَرْضِ.

فَتَحَ يوسُفُ الجَرَّةَ لِيَجِدَ أَنَّها تَحْتَوي عَلى جِنِّيٍّ قَديمٍ وَمُشاغِبٍ. قالَ الجِنِّيُّ لِيوسُفَ: "أَنا مُحْتَجَزٌ في هَذِهِ الجَرَّةِ مُنذُ قُرونٍ طَويلَةٍ. أَشْكُرُكَ عَلى تَحْريري! وَلَكِنْ عَلَيَّ أَنْ أُحَذِّرَكَ، فَأَنا جِنِّيٌّ مُشاغِبٌ وَسَأُحاوِلُ خِداعَكَ. سَأَمْنَحُكَ ثَلاثَ أُمْنِيّاتٍ، لَكِنْ عَلَيْكَ أَنْ تَكونَ حَذِرًا وَتُفَكِّرَ جَيِّدًا قَبْلَ أَنْ تَطْلُبَ شَيْئًا."

كانَ يوسُفُ رَجُلًا حَكيمًا وَذَكِيًّا وَقَرَّرَ أَنْ يَسْتَخْدِمَ أُمْنِياتِهِ بِحَذَرٍ. طَلَبَ أَوَّلًا أَنْ يَكونَ غَنِيًّا حَتّى يَتَمَكَّنَ مِنْ تَوْفيرِ حَياةٍ أَفْضَلَ لِعائِلَتِهِ. مَنَحَهُ الجِنِّيُّ الكَثيرَ مِنَ الذَّهَبِ وَالجَواهِرِ الَّتي حَوَّلَتْ حَياةَ يوسُفَ وَعائِلَتِهِ إِلى حَياةٍ مُرَفَّهَةٍ.

بَعْدَ ذَلِكَ، طَلَبَ يوسُفُ مِنَ الجِنِّيِّ أَنْ يَمْنَحَ قَرْيَتَهُ مِياهاً نَقِيَّةً وَوَفيرَةً لِلشُّرْبِ وَالرَّيِّ. قامَ الجِنِّيُّ بِتَحْقيقِ هَذِهِ الأُمْنِيَّةِ أَيْضًا، وَظَهَرَ نَبْعٌ جَديدٌ في القَرْيَةِ تَدَفَّقَتْ مِنْهُ المِياهُ النَّقِيَّةُ وَالمُنْعِشَةُ.

وَأَخيرًا، طَلَبَ يوسُفُ مِنَ الجِنِّيِّ أَنْ يَمْنَحَهُ حِكْمَةً وَفَهْمًا أَعْمَقَ لِمُساعَدَةِ أَهْلِ قَرْيَتِهِ وَحِمايَتِهِمْ مِنَ الأَخْطارِ. وافَقَ الجِنِّيُّ وَمَنَحَ يوسُفَ الحِكْمَةَ وَالفَهْمَ الَّذي طَلَبَهُ.

بِفَضْلِ حِكْمَتِهِ الجَديدَةِ، اِسْتَطاعَ يوسُفُ مُساعَدَةَ القَرَوِيّينَ في حَلِّ مَشاكِلِهِمْ وَإيجادِ حُلولٍ مُبْتَكَرَةٍ لِلتَّحَدِّياتِ الَّتي واجَهَتْهُمْ. وَمَعَ مُرورِ الوَقْتِ، أَصْبَحَ يوسُفُ شَخْصِيَّةً مُحْتَرَمَةً وَمَقْدَّرَةً في قَرْيَتِهِ.

وَلَكِنَّ الجِنِّيَّ لَمْ يَكُنْ سَعيدًا لِأَنَّهُ لَمْ يَتَمَكَّنْ مِنْ خِداعِ يوسُفَ بِأُمْنِياتِهِ الثَّلاثِ. قَرَّرَ الجِنِّيُّ أَنْ يُحاوِلَ خِداعَ يوسُفَ بِطُرُقٍ أُخْرى. بَدَأَ الجِنِّيُّ في إِحْداثِ المَشاكِلِ وَالفَوْضى في القَرْيَةِ، كَتَدْميرِ المَحاصيلِ وَإِطْلاقِ النّارِ عَلى المَنازِلِ وَإِثارَةِ المُشاجَراتِ بَيْنَ القَرَوِيّينَ.

اِسْتَخْدَمَ يوسُفُ حِكْمَتَهُ وَفَهْمَهُ لِإِصْلاحِ الأَضْرارِ الَّتي سَبَّبَها الجِنِّيُّ

وَتَهْدِئَةِ المَواقِفِ المُتَوَتِّرَةُ بَيْنَ القَرَوِيِّينَ. وَمَعَ مُرورِ الوَقْتِ، بَدَأَ الجَنِّيُّ يُدْرِكُ أَنَّهُ لَنْ يَتَمَكَّنَ مِنْ خِداعِ يوسُفَ، وَأَنَّهُ قَدْ تَمَكَّنَ مِنَ التَّغَلُّبِ عَلى مَكْرِهِ بِذَكائِهِ وَحِكْمَتِهِ.

في النِّهايَةِ، قَرَّرَ الجِنِّيُّ أَنْ يَتْرُكَ يوسُفَ وَقَرْيَتَهُ في سَلامٍ، وَأَنْ يَذْهَبَ بَحْثًا عَنْ شَخْصٍ آخَرَ يُمْكِنُهُ خِداعُهُ. وَعَلى الرَّغْمِ مِنْ رَحيلِ الجِنِّيِّ، اسْتَمَرَّتْ حِكْمَةُ يوسُفَ في مُساعَدَةِ القَرَوِيِّينَ وَتَحْسينِ حَياتِهِمْ.

بَعْدَ سَماعِ المَلِكِ شَهْرَيارَ لِقِصَّةِ الفَلّاحِ الذَّكِيِّ وَالجِنِّيِّ المُشاغِبِ، أَصْبَحَ مُتَحَمِّسًا لِسَماعِ المَزيدِ مِنَ القِصَصِ الرّائِعَةِ وَالمُلْهِمَةِ الَّتي تَحْمِلُ دُروسًا قَيِّمَةً. وَهَكَذا، انْتَظَرَ بِفارِغِ الصَّبْرِ بَدْءَ القِصَّةِ التّالِيَةِ الَّتي سَتَرْويها شَهْرَزادُ.

Questions

1. ماذا وَجَدَ يوسُفُ عِنْدَما اصْطَدَمَ مِعْوَلُهُ بِجَرَّةٍ غَريبَةٍ مَدْفونَةٍ تَحْتَ الأَرْضِ؟

2. كَمْ عَدَدُ الأُمْنِيّاتِ الَّتي مَنَحَها الجِنِّيُّ ليوسُفَ وَماذا كانَتْ تِلْكَ الأُمْنِيّاتُ؟

3. كَيْفَ اسْتَخْدَمَ يوسُفُ الحِكْمَةَ الَّتي مَنَحَها لَهُ الجِنِّيُّ؟

4. ماذا فَعَلَ الجِنِّيُّ عِنْدَما لَمْ يَتَمَكَّنْ مِنْ خِداعِ يوسُفَ بِطَلَباتِهِ الثَّلاثَةِ؟

5. ماذا فَعَلَ يوسُفُ لِمُواجَهَةِ المَشاكِلِ الَّتي سَبَّبَها الجِنِّيُّ في القَرْيَةِ؟

Answers

١. وَجَدَ يوسُفُ جِنِّيًّا قَديمًا وَمُشاغِبًا مُحْتَجَزًا داخِلَ الجَرَّة.

٢. الإِجابَةُ : مَنَحَ الجِنِّيُّ يوسُفَ ثَلاثَ أُمْنِيّاتِ: أَنْ يُصْبِحَ غَنِيًّا، وَأَنْ يَمْنَحَ قَرْيَتَهُ مِياهً نَقِيَّةً وَوَفيرَةً، وَأَنْ يَمْنَحَهُ حِكْمَةً وَفَهْمًا أَعْمَقَ .

٣. اِسْتَخْدَمَ يوسُفُ الحِكْمَةَ لِمُساعَدَةِ القَرَوِيّينَ في حَلِّ مَشاكِلِهِمْ وَإِيجادِ حُلولٍ مُبْتَكَرَةٍ لِلتَّحَدِّياتِ الَّتي واجَهَتْهُمْ.

٤. قَرَّرَ الجِنِّيُّ أَنْ يُحاوِلَ خِداعَ يوسُفَ بِطُرُقٍ أُخْرى وَبَدَأَ في إِحْداثِ المَشاكِلِ وَالفَوْضى في القَرْيَةِ.

٥. اِسْتَخْدَمَ يوسُفُ حِكْمَتَهُ وَفَهْمَهُ لِإِصْلاحِ الأَضْرارِ الَّتي سَبَّبَها الجِنِّيُّ وَتَهْدِئَةِ المَواقِفِ المُتَوَتِّرَةِ بَيْنَ القَرَوِيّينَ.

Chapter 6: The Clever Farmer and the Mischievous Genie

On the following night, Scheherazade began telling another story to King Shahryar about a clever farmer and a mischievous genie.

There was a poor farmer named Youssef who lived in a small village. Youssef worked hard to provide for his family and make ends meet. One sunny day, he decided to go to the field to pick some fruits and vegetables to sell at the market. While plowing the land, his plow hit a strange jar buried in the ground.

Youssef opened the jar to find an old and mischievous genie inside. The genie said to Youssef, "I have been trapped in this jar for centuries. Thank you for freeing me! But I must warn you, I am a mischievous genie, and I will try to deceive you. I will grant you three wishes, but you must be careful and think carefully before you ask for anything."

Youssef was a wise and clever man and decided to use his wishes carefully. He first wished to be rich so that he could provide a better life for his family. The genie granted him a lot of gold and jewels that turned Youssef and his family's life into a luxurious one.

Then, Youssef asked the genie to provide his village with clean and abundant water for drinking and irrigation. The genie also granted this wish, and a new spring appeared in the village that flowed with clean and refreshing water.

Finally, Youssef asked the genie to grant him wisdom and deeper understanding to help his village people and protect them from danger. The genie agreed and gave Youssef the wisdom and understanding he asked for.

With his new wisdom, Youssef was able to help the villagers solve their problems and find innovative solutions to the challenges they faced. Over time, Youssef became a respected and appreciated figure in his village.

However, the genie was not happy that he could not deceive Youssef with his three wishes. He decided to try to deceive Youssef in other ways. The genie began causing problems and chaos in the village, such as destroying crops, setting fire to homes, and inciting fights among villagers.

Youssef used his wisdom and understanding to fix the damage caused by the genie and calm the tense situations among the villagers. Over time, the genie realized that he could not deceive Youssef and that he had been defeated by his intelligence and wisdom.

In the end, the genie decided to leave Youssef and his village in peace and go in search of another person he could deceive. Despite the genie's departure, Youssef's wisdom continued to help the villagers and improve their lives.

After hearing the story of the clever farmer and the mischievous genie, King Shahryar became eager to hear more wonderful and inspiring stories that carry valuable lessons. And so, he eagerly awaited the start of the next story that Scheherazade would tell.

Questions

1. What did Youssef find when his plow collided with a strange jar buried underground?
2. How many wishes did the genie grant Youssef, and what were those wishes?
3. How did Youssef use the wisdom that the genie gave him?
4. What did the genie do when he couldn't deceive Youssef with his three requests?
5. What did Youssef do to confront the problems caused by the genie in the village?

Answers

1. Youssef found an old and mischievous genie trapped inside the jar.
2. The genie granted Youssef three wishes: to become rich, to provide his village with pure and abundant

water, and to give him wisdom and deeper understanding.

3. Youssef used the wisdom to help the villagers solve their problems and find innovative solutions to the challenges they faced.

4. The genie decided to try to deceive Youssef in other ways and began to cause problems and chaos in the village.

5. Youssef used his wisdom and understanding to repair the damage caused by the genie and calm the tense situations among the villagers.

الفَصْلُ السّابِعُ
لِصُّ الإِسْكَنْدَرِيَّةِ وَرَئِيسُ الشُّرْطَةِ

في اللَّيْلَةِ التّالِيَةِ، بَدَأَتْ شَهْرَزادُ تَرْوي قِصَّةَ لِصِّ الإِسْكَنْدَرِيَّةِ وَرَئِيسِ الشُّرْطَةِ لِلْمَلِكِ شَهْرَيارَ.

في مَدينَةِ الإِسْكَنْدَرِيَّةِ العَريقَةِ، كانَ هُناكَ لِصٌّ ماهِرٌ وَماكِرٌ يُدْعى ياسِرًا، يَقومُ بِسَرِقَةِ ثَرَواتِ النّاسِ الأَثْرِياءِ دونَ أَنْ يَتِمَّ القَبْضُ عَلَيْهِ.

كانَ ياسِرٌ يُخَطِّطُ بِعِنايَةٍ لِكُلِّ عَمَلِيَّةِ سَرِقَةٍ، حَيْثُ كانَ يَقومُ بِدِراسَةِ البُيوتِ وَالنَّشاطِ اليَوْمِيِّ لِلضَّحايا قَبْلَ تَنْفيذِ مُخَطَّطاتِه.

في أَحَدِ الأَيّامِ، سَرَقَ ياسِرٌ مَنْزِلَ تاجِرٍ ثَرِيٍّ. اِسْتَيْقَظَ التّاجِرُ لِيَجِدَ أَنَّ جَميعَ مُمْتَلَكاتِهِ الثَّمينَةِ قَدِ اخْتَفَتْ بِلا أَثَرٍ. فَوْرًا، تَوَجَّهَ إِلى رَئيسِ الشُّرْطَةِ، وَهُوَ رَجُلٌ حَكيمٌ وَصارِمٌ يُدْعى عَبْدَ الرَّحْمَنِ، لِيُبَلِّغَهُ بِالْحادِثَةِ. قالَ التّاجِرُ: "لَقَدْ سُرِقَتْ ثَرْوَتي كُلُّها! لا يُمْكِنُ أَنْ يَكونَ هَذا سِوى أَحَدِ أَفْعالِ لِصِّ الإِسْكَنْدَرِيَّةِ الشَّهيرِ."

أَثارَتْ قُدُراتُ اللِّصِّ الخارِقَةُ فُضولَ رَئيسِ الشُّرْطَةِ عَبْدِ الرَّحْمَنِ، الَّذي قَرَّرَ أَنْ يَضَعَ حَدًّا لِهَذِهِ السَّرِقاتِ وَيَقْبِضَ عَلى اللِّصِّ بِنَفْسِهِ. بَدَأَ عَبْدُ الرَّحْمَنِ بِالتَّحْقيقِ وَجَمْعِ المَعْلوماتِ حَوْلَ السَّرِقاتِ وَالبَحْثِ عَنْ تَفاصيلَ قَدْ تُساعِدُهُ عَلى الوُصولِ إِلى اللِّصِّ.

في إِحْدى اللَّيالي، اِكْتَشَفَ عَبْدُ الرَّحْمَنِ أَنَّ اللِّصَّ يَعْتَزِمُ سَرِقَةَ قَصْرِ أَحَدِ النُّبَلاءِ. قَرَّرَ عَبْدُ الرَّحْمَنِ التَّرَبُّصَ لَهُ. وَعِنْدَ مُنْتَصَفِ اللَّيْلِ،

رَأَى عَبْدُ الرَّحْمَنِ يَاسِرًا يَتَسَلَّلُ إِلَى القَصْرِ مُسْتَخْدِمًا حَبْلًا لِتَسَلُّقِ الجِدَارِ.

عِنْدَما دَخَلَ يَاسِرٌ القَصْرَ، وَجَدَ عَبْدَ الرَّحْمَنِ يَنْتَظِرُهُ بِصَبْرٍ. قَالَ عَبْدُ الرَّحْمَنِ بِصَوْتٍ هَادِئٍ: "لَقَدِ انْتَهَتْ مُغَامَرَاتُكَ يَا يَاسِرُ، أَنْتَ الآنَ بَيْنَ يَدَيْ رَئِيسِ الشُّرْطَةِ."

فُوجِئَ يَاسِرٌ بِوُجُودِ عَبْدِ الرَّحْمَنِ، لَكِنَّهُ لَمْ يَسْتَسْلِمْ بِسُهُولَةٍ. قَالَ يَاسِرٌ: "رُبَّما كُنْتُ مَحْظُوظًا هَذِهِ المَرَّةَ، لَكِنْ لَنْ تَتَمَكَّنَ مِنَ القَبْضِ عَلَى جَمِيعِ اللُّصُوصِ فِي الإِسْكَنْدَرِيَّةِ."

أَجَابَ عَبْدُ الرَّحْمَنِ بِثِقَةٍ: "قَدْ يَكُونُ ذَلِكَ صَحِيحًا، لَكِنِ اليَوْمَ سَأَتَمَكَّنُ مِنَ القَبْضِ عَلَى أَكْثَرِهِمْ شُهْرَةً وَمَكْرًا."

تَمَكَّنَ عَبْدُ الرَّحْمَنِ مِنَ القَبْضِ عَلَى يَاسِرٍ بَعْدَ مُطَارَدَةٍ قَصِيرَةٍ دَاخِلَ القَصْرِ. أُلْقِيَ القَبْضُ عَلَى يَاسِرٍ وَأُدِينَ بِجَمِيعِ جَرَائِمِهِ. فِي المَحْكَمَةِ، سَأَلَ القَاضِي يَاسِرًا: "لِمَاذَا قَرَّرْتَ أَنْ تَكُونَ لِصًّا وَتَسْرِقَ مِنَ النَّاسِ بَدَلًا مِنْ كَسْبِ قُوتِكَ بِشَكْلٍ شَرْعِيٍّ؟"

أَجَابَ يَاسِرٌ: "كُنْتُ فَقِيرًا وَلَمْ يَكُنْ لَدَيَّ مَهَارَاتٌ أَوْ تَعْلِيمٌ يُمَكِّنُنِي

مِنَ العَيْشِ بِكَرامَةٍ. لَمْ أَكُنْ أَرْغَبُ في إيذاءِ أَحَدٍ، لَكِنَّ الظُّروفَ جَعَلَتْني أَختارُ هَذا المَصيرَ."

أَدْرَكَ عَبْدُ الرَّحْمَنِ أَنَّ الظُّروفَ القاسِيَةَ كانَتِ السَّبَبَ الرَّئيسِيَّ وَراءَ اخْتِيارِ ياسِرٍ لِحَياةِ الجَريمَةِ. قَرَّرَ عَبْدُ الرَّحْمَنِ أَنْ يُساعِدَ ياسِرًا عَلى تَغْييرِ حَياتِهِ وَأَنْ يَمْنَحَهُ فُرْصَةً لِكَيْ يُصْبِحَ شَخْصًا أَفْضَلَ. بَعْدَ قَضاءِ ياسِرٍ فَتْرَةَ عُقوبَتِهِ، وَفَّرَ عَبْدُ الرَّحْمَنِ لَهُ فُرْصَةَ عَمَلٍ كَحارِسٍ لِمَنْزِلِ أَحَدِ التُّجّارِ الأَثْرِياءِ.

اِنْتَهَتْ شَهْرَزادُ مِنْ سَرْدِ قِصَّةِ لِصِّ الإِسْكَنْدَرِيَّةِ وَرَئيسِ الشُّرْطَةِ. كانَ المَلِكُ شَهْرَيارُ مُعْجَبًا بِهَذِهِ القِصَّةِ وَأَرادَ سَماعَ المَزيدِ مِنَ القِصَصِ المُلْهِمَةِ وَالمُثيرَةِ. وَهَكَذا، أَرْغَمَتْ شَهْرَزادُ المَلِكَ شَهْرَيارَ عَلى الاِنْتِظارِ حَتّى اللَّيْلَةِ التّالِيَةِ لِسَماعِ قِصَّةٍ أُخْرى.

عَلَّمَتْ هَذِهِ القِصَّةُ المَلِكَ شَهْرَيارَ وَالنّاسَ الَّذينَ سَمِعوها أَنَّ الظُّروفَ القاسِيَةَ يُمْكِنُ أَنْ تُجْبِرَ البَعْضَ عَلى ارْتِكابِ أَفْعالٍ سَيِّئَةٍ، وَلَكِنْ لا يَزالُ هُناكَ أَمَلٌ لِإِعادَةِ تَوْجِيهِ حَياتِهِمْ وَالسَّعْيِ نَحْوَ

مُسْتَقْبَلٍ أَفْضَلَ بِمُساعَدَةِ الآخَرينَ. تَذَكَّرَ المَلِكُ أَنَّ العَدْلَ وَالرَّحْمَةَ يَجِبُ أَنْ يَسودا في حُكْمِهِ، وَأَنَّهُ يَنْبَغي أَنْ يَكونَ مُسْتَعِدًّا لِتَوْفيرِ فُرَصٍ ثانِيَةٍ لِلْمُسْتَضْعَفينَ في مَمْلَكَتِهِ.

Questions

1. ما اسْمُ اللِّصِّ الَّذي كانَ يَسْرِقُ ثَرَواتِ النّاسِ الأَثْرِياءِ في الإِسْكَنْدَرِيَّةِ؟

2. ماذا كانَ ياسِرٌ يَفْعَلُ قَبْلَ تَنْفيذِ مُخَطَّطاتِ السَّرِقَةِ؟

3. مَنْ هُوَ رَئيسُ الشُّرْطَةِ الَّذي قَرَّرَ أَنْ يَضَعَ حَدّاً لِسَرِقاتِ ياسِرٍ؟

4. كَيْفَ تَمَكَّنَ عَبْدُ الرَّحْمَنِ مِنَ القَبْضِ عَلى ياسِرٍ؟

5. كَيْفَ ساعَدَ عَبْدُ الرَّحْمَنِ ياسِراً بَعْدَ قَضاءِ فَتْرَةِ عُقوبَتِهِ؟

Answers

1. اِسْمُ اللِّصِّ هُوَ ياسِرٌ.

2. كانَ ياسِرٌ يُخَطِّطُ بِعِنايَةٍ لِكُلِّ عَمَلِيَّةِ سَرِقَةٍ، حَيْثُ كانَ يَقومُ بِدِراسَةِ البُيوتِ وَالنَّشاطِ اليَوْمِيِّ لِلضَّحايا.

3. عَبْدُ الرَّحْمَنِ هُوَ رَئيسُ الشُّرْطَةِ الَّذي قَرَّرَ ذَلِكَ.

4. اِكْتَشَفَ عَبْدُ الرَّحْمَنِ أَنَّ اللِّصَّ يَعْتَزِمُ سَرِقَةَ قَصْرِ أَحَدِ النُّبَلاءِ وَتَرَبَّصَ بِهِ.

5. وَفَّرَ عَبْدُ الرَّحْمَنِ لَهُ فُرْصَةَ عَمَلٍ كَحارِسٍ لِمَنْزِلِ أَحَدِ التُّجّارِ الأَثْرِياءِ.

Chapter 7: The Thief of Alexandria and the Police Chief

The next night, Scheherazade began to tell the story of the Alexandria Thief and the Chief of Police to King Shahryar.

In the ancient city of Alexandria, there was a skilled and cunning thief named Yaser who robbed the wealth of rich people without being caught. Yaser planned carefully for each theft, and he studied the houses and daily schedules of his victims before executing his plans.

One day, Yaser stole from the house of a wealthy merchant. The merchant woke up to find that all his valuable possessions had disappeared without a trace. Immediately, he went to the Chief of Police, a wise and strict man named Abdulrahman, to report the incident. The merchant said, "All my wealth has been stolen! This can only be the work of the notorious Thief of Alexandria."

The extraordinary abilities of the thief intrigued the Chief of Police, Abdulrahman, who decided to put an end to these thefts and capture the thief himself. Abdulrahman began investigating and gathering information about the thefts and searching for details that could help him reach the thief.

One night, Abdulrahman discovered that the thief was planning to steal the palace of a nobleman. Abdulrahman decided to wait for him in ambush. And at midnight,

Abdulrahman saw Yaser sneaking into the palace and using a rope to climb the wall.

When Yaser entered the palace, he found Abdulrahman waiting for him patiently. Abdulrahman said calmly, "Your adventures have come to an end, Yaser. You are now in the hands of the Chief of Police."

Yaser was surprised by the presence of Abdulrahman, but he did not surrender easily. He said, "Maybe you were lucky this time, but you won't be able to catch all the thieves in Alexandria."

Abdulrahman answered confidently, "It may be true, but today I will be able to catch the most famous and cunning of them."

Abdulrahman managed to catch Yaser after a short chase inside the palace. Yaser was arrested and convicted of all his crimes. In court, the judge asked Yaser, "Why did you decide to become a thief and steal from people instead of earning your living legally?"

Yaser answered, "I was poor and had no skills or education that could enable me to live with dignity. I didn't want to hurt anyone, but circumstances forced me to choose this fate."

Abdulrahman realized that harsh circumstances were the main reason behind Yaser's choice of a life of crime. He decided to help Yaser change his life and provide him with an opportunity to become a better person. After Yaser served his sentence, Abdulrahman provided him with a job opportunity as a guard in a a wealthy merchant's house.

Scheherazade finished telling the story of the Alexandria thief and the police chief. King Shahryar was impressed by this story and wanted to hear more inspiring and exciting stories. Thus, Scheherazade forced King Shahryar to wait until the next night to hear another story.

This story taught King Shahryar and the people who heard it that harsh circumstances could force some people to commit bad deeds, but there is still hope to redirect their lives and work towards a better future with the help of others. The king remembered that justice and mercy should prevail in his rule and that he should be prepared to provide second chances to the less fortunate in his kingdom.

Questions

1. What is the name of the thief who was stealing the wealth of rich people in Alexandria?
2. What was Yaser doing before carrying out his robbery plans?
3. Who is the police chief who decided to put an end to Yaser's robberies?
4. How did Abdulrahman manage to arrest Yaser?

5. How did Abdulrahman help Yaser after he served his sentence?

Answers

1. Yaser is the name of the thief.
2. Yaser was carefully planning each robbery, where he would study the houses and the daily schedules of his victims.
3. Abdulrahman is the police chief who made that decision.
4. Abdulrahman discovered that the thief planned to steal from the palace of a nobleman and waited for him in an ambush.
5. Abdulrahman provided him with a job opportunity as a guard in a a wealthy merchant's house.

الفَصْلُ الثّامِنُ
الطّائِرُ الأَزْرَقُ

في اللَّيْلَةِ التّالِيَةِ، بَدَأَتْ شَهْرَزادُ تَرْوي قِصَّةَ الطّائِرِ الأَزْرَقِ لِلْمَلِكِ شَهْرَيارَ.

في بِلادٍ بَعيدَةٍ، كانَ هُناكَ مَلِكٌ طَيِّبٌ وَزَوْجَتُهُ المَلِكَةُ. كانَ لَدَيْهِما ابْنَةٌ جَميلَةٌ اسْمُها الأَميرَةُ لَيْلى. عَلى الرَّغْمِ مِنْ جَمالِها وَنُبْلِها،

كانَتْ لَيْلى تَشْعُرُ بِالْحُزْنِ لِأَنَّها لَمْ تَجِدْ حُبَّ حَياتِها. في يَوْمٍ مِنَ الأَيّامِ، أَثْناءَ تَجَوُّلِها في حَديقَةِ القَصْرِ، سَمِعْتْ تَغْريدَ طائِرٍ جَميلٍ ذي لَوْنٍ أَزْرَقَ زاهٍ. لَمْ يَرَ أَحَدٌ مِثْلَ هَذا الطّائِرِ مِنْ قِبَلُ.

فَكَّرَتِ الأَميرَةُ لَيْلى أَنَّ هَذا الطّائِرَ الأَزْرَقَ يُمْكِنُ أَنْ يَكونَ مِفْتاحَ سَعادَتِها، فَقَرَّرَتِ البَحْثَ عَنْهُ. طَلَبَتْ مِنْ والِدِها المَلِكِ أَنْ يُعْلِنَ مُسابَقَةً، حَيْثُ يَتَعَيَّنُ عَلى المُشْتَرِكينَ البَحْثُ عَنِ الطّائِرِ الأَزْرَقِ وَإِحْضارُهُ لَها. وافَقَ المَلِكُ عَلى الفِكْرَةِ وَأَعْلَنَ المُسابَقَةَ لِجَميعِ شَبابِ المَمْلَكَةِ.

تَوافَدَ العَديدُ مِنَ الشَّبابِ عَلى القَصْرِ لِلْمُشارَكَةِ في المُسابَقَةِ وَالبَحْثِ عَنِ الطّائِرِ الأَزْرَقِ. بَيْنَ المُشارِكينَ، كانَ هُناكَ شابٌّ فَقيرٌ اسْمُهُ ياسينُ. كانَ ياسينُ مُغْرَمًا بِالأَميرَةِ لَيْلى وَأَرادَ إِسْعادَها بِجَلْبِ الطّائِرِ الأَزْرَقِ. لَمْ يَكُنْ يَمْلِكُ الثَّرْوَةَ أَوِ المَنْصِبَ لِيَكونَ مُلائِمًا لِلْأَميرَةِ، لَكِنَّهُ كانَ يَتَمَتَّعُ بِالذَّكاءِ وَالشَّجاعَةِ وَالإِصْرارِ.

بَدَأَ ياسينُ رِحْلَتَهُ الطَّويلَةَ بَحْثًا عَنِ الطّائِرِ الأَزْرَقِ. مَرَّتِ الأَيّامُ وَالأَسابيعُ وَالأَشْهُرُ دونَ جَدْوى. في هَذِهِ الرِّحْلَةِ، واجَهَ العَديدَ مِنْ

التَّحَدِّياتِ والمَخاطِرِ، لَكِنَّهُ لَمْ يَسْتَسْلِمْ. أَثْناءَ رِحْلَتِهِ، التَقى ياسينُ بِالعَديدِ مِنَ الأشْخاصِ الَّذينَ ساعَدوهُ وَأَوْصَلوهُ إلى مَعْلوماتٍ جَديدَةٍ عَنْ مَكانِ وُجودِ الطّائِرِ الأَزْرَقِ.

في النِّهايَةِ، اِكْتَشَفَ ياسينُ أَنَّ الطّائِرَ الأَزْرَقَ يَعيشُ في جَزيرَةٍ نائِيَةٍ وَسَطَ البَحْرِ. قَرَّرَ ياسينُ أَنْ يُبْحِرَ إلى هَذِهِ الجَزيرَةِ لِيَجِدَ الطّائِرَ وَيَعودَ بِهِ إلى الأميرَةِ لَيْلى. بَعْدَ أَيّامٍ طَويلَةٍ مِنَ المُعاناةِ والعَواصِفِ البَحْرِيَّةِ العَنيفَةِ، وَصَلَ ياسينُ إلى الجَزيرَةِ النّائِيَةِ.

اِسْتَكْشَفَ ياسينُ الجَزيرَةَ، وَواجَهَ العَديدَ مِنَ العَقَباتِ والمَخْلوقاتِ الغَريبَةِ، لَكِنَّهُ لَمْ يَسْتَسْلِمْ. بَعْدَ بَحْثٍ شاقٍّ وَمُثابَرَةٍ، وَجَدَ ياسينُ الطّائِرَ الأَزْرَقَ وَتَمَكَّنَ مِنَ الإمْساكِ بِهِ. بِفَرْحَةٍ كَبيرَةٍ، عادَ ياسينُ بِالطّائِرِ الأَزْرَقِ إلى المَمْلَكَةِ.

عِنْدَما عادَ ياسينُ وَأَظْهَرَ الطّائِرَ الأَزْرَقَ لِلأميرَةِ لَيْلى، اِمْتَلَأَتْ قُلوبُ الجَميعِ بِالسُّرورِ والدَّهْشَةِ. اِحْتَفَلَ المَلِكُ بِعَوْدَةِ ياسينَ وَأَعْلَنَ فَوْزَهُ في المُسابَقَةِ. لَكِنَّ الأميرَةَ لَيْلى لَمْ تَكُنْ تَرْغَبُ فَقَطْ في الطّائِرِ

الأَزْرَقِ، بَلْ أَيْضًا فِي الشَّابِّ الَّذِي ذَهَبَ إِلَى نِهَايَةِ العَالَمِ مِنْ أَجْلِهَا.

تَزَوَّجَتِ الأَمِيرَةُ لَيْلَى مِنْ يَاسِينَ بِمُوَافَقَةِ المَلِكِ وَالمَلِكَةِ. عَاشَ يَاسِينُ وَالأَمِيرَةُ لَيْلَى حَيَاةً سَعِيدَةً مَلِيئَةً بِالْحُبِّ وَالرَّفَاهِيَةِ. وَعَلَّمَتِ القِصَّةُ المَلِكَ شَهْرَيَارَ وَالنَّاسَ أَنَّ الإِصْرَارَ وَالشَّجَاعَةَ وَالحُبَّ يُمْكِنُهُمُ التَّغَلُّبُ عَلَى أَيِّ تَحَدٍّ وَالمُسَاعَدَةُ عَلَى الوُصُولِ إِلَى السَّعَادَةِ الحَقِيقِيَّةِ.

وَهَكَذَا، انْتَهَى الفَصْلُ الثَّامِنُ مِنْ حِكَايَاتِ الأَلْفِ لَيْلَةٍ وَلَيْلَةٍ. لَمْ يَتَسَنَّ لِلْمَلِكِ شَهْرَيَارَ إِلَّا الاِنْتِظَارُ بِفَارِغِ الصَّبْرِ حَتَّى اللَّيْلَةِ التَّالِيَةِ لِيَسْتَمْتِعَ بِقِصَّةٍ جَدِيدَةٍ تَرْوِيهَا لَهُ شَهْرَزَادُ.

فِي اللَّيْلَةِ التَّالِيَةِ، اجْتَمَعَ المَلِكُ شَهْرَيَارُ وَشَهْرَزَادُ مَرَّةً أُخْرَى، حَيْثُ كَانَ المَلِكُ مُتَشَوِّقًا لِسَمَاعِ المَزِيدِ مِنَ القِصَصِ المُلْهِمَةِ وَالمُثِيرَةِ. شَعَرَ المَلِكُ شَهْرَيَارُ بِأَنَّ هَذِهِ الحِكَايَاتِ قَدْ غَيَّرَتْ حَيَاتَهُ لِلْأَفْضَلِ، وَأَنَّهَا عَلَّمَتْهُ دُرُوسًا قَيِّمَةً عَنِ العَدْلِ وَالحِكْمَةِ وَالحُبِّ.

وَعَلَى هَذَا المِنْوَالِ، اسْتَمَرَّتْ شَهْرَزَادُ فِي سَرْدِ قِصَصِهَا لِلْمَلِكِ شَهْرَيَارَ

لَيْلَةً بَعْدَ لَيْلَةٍ، مُحاوِلَةً تَعْلِيمَهُ وَشَعْبَهُ المَزِيدَ مِنَ الدُّروسِ الهامَّةِ عَنِ الحَياةِ وَالإِنْسانِيَّةِ.

Questions

1. بِمَ كانَتِ الأَميرَةُ لَيْلى تَشْعُرُ؟ وَلِماذا؟

2. ما الَّذي طَلَبَتْهُ الأَميرَةُ لَيْلى مِنْ والِدِها المَلِكِ؟

3. مِنْ هُوَ ياسينُ؟ وَما الَّذي جَعَلَهُ يُشارِكُ في المُسابَقَةِ؟

4. أَيْنَ عَلِمَ ياسينُ أَنَّ الطّائِرَ الأَزْرَقَ يَعيشُ؟

5. ماذا حَدَثَ عِنْدَما عادَ ياسينُ بِالطّائِرِ الأَزْرَقِ إِلى المَمْلَكَةِ؟

Answers

1. كانَتِ الأميرَةُ لَيْلى تَشْعُرُ بِالْحُزْنِ لِأَنَّها لَمْ تَجِدْ حُبَّ حَياتِها.

2. طَلَبَتِ الأميرَةُ لَيْلى مِنْ والِدِها المَلِكِ أَنْ يُعْلِنَ مُسابَقَةً لِلْبَحْثِ عَنِ الطّائِرِ الأَزْرَقِ وَإِحْضارِهِ لَها.

3. ياسينُ هُوَ شابٌّ فَقيرٌ كانَ مُغْرَمًا بِالأميرَةِ لَيْلى، وَأَرادَ إِسْعادَها بِجَلْبِ الطّائِرِ الأَزْرَقِ لها.

4. عَلِمَ ياسينُ أَنَّ الطّائِرَ الأَزْرَقَ يَعيشُ في جَزيرَةٍ نائِيَةٍ وَسَطَ البَحْرِ.

5. اِمْتَلَأَتْ قُلوبُ الجَميعِ بِالسُّرورِ والدَّهْشَةِ عِنْدَ عَوْدَةِ ياسينَ بِالطّائِرِ الأَزْرَقِ، واحْتَفَلَ المَلِكُ بِفَوْزِهِ في المُسابَقَةِ، وَتَزَوَّجَتِ الأميرَةُ لَيْلى مِنْ ياسينَ.

Chapter 8: The Blue Bird

On the following night, Scheherazade began to tell King Shahryar the story of the Blue Bird.

In a faraway land, there was a kind king and his queen. They had a beautiful daughter named Princess Leila. Despite her beauty and nobility, Leila felt unhappy because she had not yet found the love of her life. One day, while walking in the palace garden, she heard the singing of a beautiful bird with bright blue feathers. No one had ever seen a bird like this before.

Princess Leila thought that the Blue Bird might be the key to her happiness, so she decided to search for it. She asked her father, the king, to announce a contest in which all the participants must search for the Blue Bird and bring it to her. The king agreed to the idea and announced the contest to all the young men in the kingdom.

Many young men came to the palace to participate in the contest and search for the Blue Bird. Among them was a poor young man named Yassin. Yassin was in love with Princess Leila and wanted to make her happy by finding the Blue Bird. He did not have wealth or a position that would be suitable for the princess, but he had intelligence, bravery, and determination.

Yassin began his long journey to search for the Blue Bird. Days, weeks, and months passed without any success. On this journey, he faced many challenges and dangers, but he did not give up. During his journey, Yassin met many people who helped him and provided him with new information about the whereabouts of the Blue Bird.

In the end, Yassin discovered that the Blue Bird lived on a remote island in the middle of the sea. He decided to sail to this island to find the bird and bring it back to Princess Leila. After many days of suffering and violent storms at sea, Yassin arrived at the remote island.

Yassin explored the island and faced many obstacles and strange creatures, but he did not give up. After a long search and perseverance, Yassin found the Blue Bird and managed to catch it. With great joy, Yassin returned to the kingdom with the Blue Bird.

When Yassin returned and showed the Blue Bird to Princess Leila, everyone's hearts filled with happiness and amazement. The king celebrated Yassin's return and announced his victory in the contest. But Princess Leila did not only want the Blue Bird; she also wanted the young man who went to the ends of the earth to make her happy.

Princess Leila married Yassin with the approval of the king and queen. Yassin and Princess Leila lived a happy life filled with love and prosperity. The story taught King Shahryar and the people that determination, bravery, and love could overcome any challenge and lead to true happiness.

And so, the eighth chapter of the Tales of One Thousand and One Nights came to an end. King Shahryar could only wait eagerly for the next night to hear another inspiring and exciting story from Scheherazade.

On the following night, King Shahryar and Scheherazade gathered again, where the king was eager to hear more inspiring and exciting stories. King Shahryar felt that these stories had changed his life for the better and taught him valuable lessons about justice, wisdom, and love.

And so, Scheherazade continued to tell her stories to King Shahryar night after night, trying to teach him and his people more important lessons about life and humanity.

Questions

1. What was Princess Leila feeling and why?
2. What did Princess Leila ask her father, the king, for?
3. Who is Yasin, and what made him participate in the competition?
4. Where did Yasin learn that the blue bird lived?
5. What happened when Yasin returned with the blue bird to the kingdom?

6. How did people's lives improve in the kingdom after the princess's return?

Answers

1. Princess Leila was feeling sad because she had not found the love of her life.
2. Princess Leila asked her father, the king, to announce a competition to search for and bring her the blue bird.
3. Yasin is a poor young man who is in love with Princess Leila and wants to make her happy by bringing her the blue bird.
4. Yasin learned that the blue bird lived on a remote island in the middle of the sea.
5. Everyone's hearts were filled with joy and amazement when Yasin returned with the blue bird. The king celebrated his victory in the competition, and Princess Leila married Yasin.

الفَصْلُ التّاسِعُ
الفَتاةُ وَالسّاحِرَةُ

في اللَّيْلَةِ التّالِيَةِ، اِسْتَعَدَّ المَلِكُ شَهْرَيارُ لِيَسْتَمِعَ إلى قِصَّةٍ جَديدَةٍ مِنْ شَهْرَزادَ. بَدَأتْ شَهْرَزادُ تَرْوي قِصَّةَ الفَتاةِ وَالسّاحِرَةِ.

في يَوْمٍ مِنَ الأَيّامِ، في قَرْيَةٍ بَعيدَةٍ، كانَتْ هُناكَ فَتاةٌ شابَّةٌ تُدْعى لينا. كانَتْ لينا تَعيشُ مَعَ والِدَتِها المَريضَةِ وَأَخيها الصَّغيرِ. كانُوا

فُقَراءَ وَيُكافِحونَ لِتَوْفيرِ قوتِ يَوْمِهِمْ. في أَحَدِ الأَيّامِ، ذَهَبَتْ لينا إلى الغابَةِ لِجَمْعِ الفِطْرِ وَالتّوتِ لِعائِلَتِها. بَيْنَما كانَتْ تَتَجَوَّلُ في الغابَةِ، سَمِعَتْ صَوْتًا ضَعيفًا يُناديها.

تَتَبَّعَتْ لينا الصَّوْتَ حَتّى وَصَلَتْ إلى سَيِّدَةٍ مُسِنَّةٍ. كانَتِ العَجوزُ تَبْدو هَزيلَةً وَضَعيفَةً، وَكانَتْ تُحاوِلُ الاِحْتِماءَ مِنَ البَرْدِ. عِنْدَما رَأَتْ لينا حالَتَها المُزْرِيَةَ، قَرَّرَتْ مُساعَدَتَها. اِصْطَحَبَتِ الفَتاةُ العَجوزَ إلى مَنْزِلِها، حَيْثُ قَدَّمَتْ لَها الطَّعامَ وَالمَأْوى. بِالرَّغْمِ مِنَ الفَقْرِ الَّذي كانَتْ تَعيشُ فيهِ عائِلَتُها، تَحَلَّتْ لينا بِالكَرَمِ وَالعَطْفِ.

بَعْدَ أَنِ اسْتَعادَتِ العَجوزُ قُوَّتَها، كَشَفَتْ لِلينا أَنَّها في الواقِعِ ساحِرَةٌ قَوِيَّةٌ. اِمْتِنانًا لِطيبَةِ قَلْبِ لَينا وَكَرَمِها، عَرَضَتِ السّاحِرَةُ عَلى لينا مَنْحَها ثَلاثَ أُمْنِيّاتٍ. فَكَّرَتْ لينا في الأَمْرِ وَقَرَّرَتْ أَنْ تَطْلُبَ الشِّفاءَ لِوالِدَتِها، وَتَحْسينَ حَياةِ أَخيها، وَالثَّرْوَةَ لِتَوْفيرِ حَياةٍ أَفْضَلَ لِعائِلَتِها.

وافَقَتِ السّاحِرَةُ عَلى تَحْقيقِ أُمْنِيّاتِ لينا، وَقامَتْ بِتَحْويلِ حَياةِ

العائِلَةِ إلى الأَفْضَلِ. عادَتْ والِدَةُ لينا صَحيحَةً وَنَشيطَةً مَرَّةً أُخْرى، وَتَمَكَّنَ أَخوها مِنَ الذَّهابِ إلى المَدْرَسَةِ والتَّعَلُّمِ. وَبِفَضْلِ الثَّرْوَةِ الَّتي حَصَلوا عَلَيْها، اِسْتَطاعَتْ عائِلَةُ لينا أَنْ تَبْنِيَ مَنْزِلًا جَديدًا وَأَنْ تُوَفِّرَ حَياةً مُريحَةً لِأَفْرادِها.

مَرَّتِ السَّنَواتُ، وازْدَهَرَتِ العائِلَةُ بِفَضْلِ المُساعَدَةِ السِّحْرِيَّةِ. كَبُرَتْ لينا وَأَصْبَحَتْ فَتاةً جَميلَةً وَذَكِيَّةً وَشُجاعَةً. تَذَكَّرَتْ دائِمًا عَطْفَ السّاحِرَةِ عَلَيْها وَ عَلى عائِلَتِها، وَلِذَلِكَ قَرَّرَتْ أَنْ تُساعِدَ الآخَرينَ في قَرْيَتِها. أَصْبَحَتْ مَعْروفَةً بِحِكْمَتِها وَرَحْمَتِها، حَيْثُ كانَتْ تُقَدِّمُ المَشورَةَ وَالمُساعَدَةَ لِجيرانِها.

ذاتَ يَوْمٍ، اِقْتَرَبَ شابٌّ غَريبٌ مِنْ لينا وَطَلَبَ مُساعَدَتَها. كانَتِ القَرْيَةُ مُهَدَّدَةً مِنْ مَجْموعَةٍ مِنَ اللُّصوصِ الَّذينَ يَسْعَوْنَ لِسَلْبِ مُمْتَلَكاتِ النّاسِ وَتَرْويعِهِمْ. اِسْتَعانَتْ لينا بِذَكائِها وَشَجاعَتِها لِتَنْظيمِ القَرَوِيّينَ وَالتَّصَدّي لِلُّصوصِ. بَعْدَ مُواجَهَةٍ شَرِسَةٍ، تَمَكَّنوا مِنْ هَزيمَةِ اللُّصوصِ وَتَأْمينِ القَرْيَةِ.

بِفَضْلِ شَجاعَتِها وَحِكْمَتِها، أَصْبَحَتْ لينا قائِدَةً مُحْتَرَمَةً في قَرْيَتِها.

تَزَوَّجَتْ مِنَ الشّابِّ الَّذي طَلَبَ مُساعَدَتَها، وَأَسَّسا عائِلَةً جَديدَةً مَعًا. عاشَتْ لينا حَياةً سَعيدَةً وَمُسْتَقِرَّةً، وَظَلَّتْ تُساعِدُ القَرْيَةَ بِحِكْمَتِها وَقُوَّتِها. فازَتْ بَحُبِّ واحْتِرامِ جَميعِ سُكّانِ القَرْيَةِ لِما قَدَّمَتْهُ مِنْ تَضْحِياتٍ وَمُساعَداتٍ.

اِنْتَهَتْ شَهْرَزادُ مِنْ سَرْدِ قِصَّةِ الفَتاةِ وَالسّاحِرَةِ، وَكانَ المَلِكُ شَهْرَيارُ يَسْتَمِعُ بِفارِغِ الصَّبْرِ لِلْقِصَّةِ. عَلى الرَّغْمِ مِنْ كَوْنِها قِصَّةً مُخْتَلِفَةً عَنِ القِصَصِ السّابِقَةِ، لَكِنَّهُ اسْتَمْتَعَ بِها وَكانَ مُتَشَوِّقًا لِسَماعِ القِصَّةِ التّالِيَةِ.

Questions

1. ماذا كانَتْ لينا تَفْعَلُ في الغابةِ قَبْلَ أَنْ تَلْتَقِيَ بِالْعَجوزِ؟

2. كَيْفَ ساعَدَتْ لينا العَجوزَ؟

3. ماذا كَشَفَتِ العَجوزُ عَنْ نَفْسِها بَعْدَ أَنِ اسْتَعادَتْ قوَّتَها؟

4. ما الثَّلاثُ أُمنِيّاتٍ الَّتي طَلَبَتها لينا مِنَ السّاحِرَةِ؟

5. كَيْفَ أَنْقَذَتْ لينا قَرْيَتَها مِنْ مَجْموعَةِ اللُّصوصِ؟

Answers

1. كانَتْ لينا تَجْمَعُ الفِطْرَ وَالتّوتَ لِعائِلَتِها في الغابَةِ.

2. اِصْطَحَبَتْ لينا العَجوزَ إلى مَنْزِلِها وَقَدَّمَتْ لَها الطَّعامَ وَالمَأْوى.

3. كَشَفَتِ العَجوزُ أَنَّها في الواقعِ ساحِرَةٌ قَوِيَّةٌ.

4. طَلَبَتْ شِفاءَ والِدَتِها، وتَحْسينَ حَياةِ أَخيها، وَالثَّرْوَةَ لِتَوْفيرِ حَياةٍ أَفْضَلَ لِعائِلَتِها.

5. اِسْتَعانَتْ لينا بِذَكائِها وَشَجاعَتِها لِتَنْظيمِ القَرَوِيّينَ وَالتَّصَدّي لِلُّصوصِ، وَبَعْدَ مُواجَهَةٍ شَرِسَةٍ، تَمَكَّنُوا مِنْ هَزيمَةِ اللُّصوصِ وَتَأْمينِ القَرْيَةِ.

Chapter 9: The Girl and the Magical Old Woman

On the next night, King Shahryar prepared himself to listen to a new story from Scheherazade. Scheherazade began to narrate the story of the girl and the sorceress.

Once upon a time, in a faraway village, there was a young girl named Lena. Lena lived with her sick mother and younger brother. They were poor and struggled to make ends meet. One day, Lena went to the forest to gather mushrooms and berries for her family. While wandering in the forest, she heard a weak voice calling her.

Lena followed the voice until she reached an old woman. The old woman appeared frail and weak, and she was trying to shelter from the cold. When Lena saw her miserable condition, she decided to help her. The girl took the old woman to her house, where she provided her with food and shelter. Despite the poverty that her family lived in, Lena was kind and compassionate.

After the old woman regained her strength, she revealed to Lena that she was actually a powerful sorceress. In gratitude for Lena's kindness and generosity, the sorceress offered Lena three wishes. Lena thought about it and decided to ask for her mother's healing, to improve her brother's life, and wealth to provide a better life for her family.

The sorceress agreed to fulfill Lena's wishes and transformed the family's life for the better. Lena's mother became healthy and active again, and her brother was able to go to school and learn. Thanks to the wealth they acquired, Lena's family was able to build a new house and provide a comfortable life for themselves.

Years passed, and the family flourished thanks to the magical help. Lena grew up to become a beautiful, intelligent, and brave girl. She always remembered the sorceress's kindness to her and her family and therefore decided to help others in her village. She became known for her wisdom and compassion, offering advice and assistance to her neighbors.

One day, a strange young man approached Lena and asked for her help. The village was threatened by a group of thieves who sought to steal people's possessions and intimidate them. Lena used her intelligence and courage to organize the villagers and confront the thieves. After a fierce confrontation, they managed to defeat the thieves and secure the village.

Thanks to her courage and wisdom, Lena became a respected leader in her village. She married the young man who asked for her help, and they started a new family together. Lena lived a happy and stable life and continued to help the village with her wisdom and strength. She won the love and respect of all the villagers for her sacrifices and assistance.

Scheherazade finished narrating the story of the girl and the sorceress, and King Shahryar eagerly listened to the story. Although it was a different story from the previous ones, he enjoyed it and was eager to hear the next story.

Questions

1. What was Lena doing in the forest before meeting the old woman?
2. How did Lena help the old woman?
3. What did the old woman reveal about herself after regaining her strength?
4. What were the three wishes that Lena asked the sorceress for?
5. How did Lena rescue her village from the group of thieves?

Answers

1. Lena was collecting mushrooms and berries for her family in the forest.
2. Lena took he old woman to her home and provided her with food and shelter.
3. The old woman revealed that she was actually a powerful sorceress.

4. To heal her mother, improve her brother's life, and gain wealth to provide a better life for her family.

5. Lena relied on her intelligence and bravery to organize the villagers and confront the thieves, and after a fierce confrontation, they were able to defeat the thieves and secure the village.

الفَصْلُ العاشِرُ
الأَميرُ وَالتِّنّينُ

في اللَّيْلَةِ التّاليَةِ، بَدَأَتْ شَهْرَزادُ تَروي قِصَّةَ الأَميرِ وَالتِّنّينِ لِلْمَلِكِ شَهْرَيارَ.

في مَمْلَكَةٍ بَعيدَةٍ، كانَ هُناكَ أَميرٌ شابٌّ وَشُجاعٌ اسْمُهُ رامي. كانَتِ المَمْلَكَةُ تُعاني مِنْ هَجَماتٍ مُتَكَرِّرَةٍ لِتِنّينٍ ضَخْمٍ يَعيشُ في جَبَلٍ

قَرِيبٍ. كانَ التِّنّينُ يُهاجِمُ القُرى وَيَخْطِفُ الأَوْلادِ وَالبَناتِ الصِّغارَ لِيَأْكُلَهُمْ. كانَ النَّاسُ يَعيشونَ في خَوْفٍ دائِمٍ وَلا يَجْرُؤونَ عَلى التَّصَدّي لِلتِّنّينِ الضَّخْمِ.

في أَحَدِ الأَيّامِ، اِلتَقى الأَميرُ رامي بِرَجُلٍ مِنْ إِحْدى القُرى المَنْكوبَةِ. قالَ لَهُ الرَّجُلُ: "يا أَميرَنا، لَقَدْ خَطَفَ التِّنّينُ اِبْنَتي الصَّغيرَةَ وَأَصْبَحْنا نَعيشُ في خَوْفٍ لا يُطاقُ. أَتَوَسَّلُ إِلَيْكَ أَنْ تُنْقِذَنا مِنْ هَذا الوَحْشِ المُرْعِبِ."

قَرَّرَ الأَميرُ رامي أَنْ يُواجِهَ التِّنّينَ وَيُنْقِذَ شَعْبَهُ مِنْ هَذا الوَحْشِ المُرْعِبِ. قامَ بِتَجْهيزِ نَفْسِهِ بِأَفْضَلِ الأَسْلِحَةِ وَالدُّروعِ وَانْطَلَقَ في رِحْلَتِهِ إِلى جَبَلِ التِّنّينِ. خِلالَ رِحْلَتِهِ، اِلتَقى بِحَكيمٍ عَجوزٍ أَعْطاهُ سِلاحًا سِحْرِيًّا يُمَكِّنُهُ مِنْ هَزيمَةِ التِّنّينِ.

قالَ الحَكيمُ لِلْأَميرِ: "اِسْتَخْدِمْ هَذا السِّلاحَ السِّحْرِيَّ بِحَذَرٍ، فَهُوَ الوَحيدُ الَّذي يُمَكِّنُهُ هَزيمَةُ التِّنّينِ الضَّخْمِ."

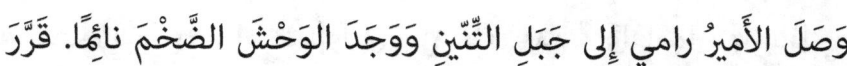

وَصَلَ الأَميرُ رامي إِلى جَبَلِ التِّنّينِ وَوَجَدَ الوَحْشَ الضَّخْمَ نائِمًا. قَرَّرَ

أَنْ يَنْتَظِرَ حَتَّى يَسْتَيْقِظَ التِّنِّينُ لِيواجِهَهُ بِشجاعةٍ. حينَ اسْتَيْقَظَ التِّنِّينُ، صَرَخَ الأَميرُ رامي قائِلًا: "يا أَيُّها التِّنِّينُ الشِّرّيرُ، سَأَقْضي عَلَيْكَ اليَوْمَ وَأُنْقِذُ شَعْبِيَ مِنْ هَجَماتِكَ الوَحْشِيّةِ!"

اِسْتَعَدَّ لِمُواجَهَةِ التِّنِّينِ، وَاسْتَخْدَمَ السِّلاحَ السِّحْرِيَّ الَّذي أَعْطاهُ لَهُ الحَكيمُ العَجوزُ. بَدَأَتِ المَعْرَكَةُ بَيْنَ الأَميرِ رامي وَالتِّنِّينِ الضَّخْمِ. كانَ التِّنِّينُ يُلَوِّحُ بِجَناحَيْهِ وَيَقْذِفُ النّارَ مِنْ فَمِهِ بِاتِّجاهِ الأَميرِ، بَيْنَما كانَ رامي يَتَفاداهُ بِبَراعَةٍ وَيَسْتَخْدِمُ سِلاحَهُ السِّحْرِيَّ لِتَوجيهِ ضَرَباتٍ قَوِيَّةٍ لِلتِّنِّينِ. تَواصَلَتِ المَعْرَكَةُ لِساعاتٍ طَويلَةٍ وَكانَ الأَميرُ رامي يَفْقِدُ قُوَّتَهُ بِبُطْءٍ.

في لَحْظَةٍ حاسِمَةٍ، اِسْتَجْمَعَ رامي كُلَّ شَجاعَتِهِ وَما تَبَقَّى لَهُ مِنْ قُوَّةٍ، وَتَمَكَّنَ مِنْ تَوجيهِ ضَرْبَةٍ قاضِيَةٍ لِلتِّنِّينِ بِاسْتِخْدامِ سِلاحِهِ السِّحْرِيِّ. سَقَطَ التِّنِّينُ أَرْضًا وَلَفَظَ أَنْفاسَهُ الأَخيرَةَ. وَبِذلِكَ أَنْقَذَ الأَميرُ رامي شَعْبَهُ مِنَ الوَحْشِ المُرْعِبِ.

عادَ الأَميرُ رامي إِلى المَمْلَكَةِ، حَيْثُ انْتَظَرَهُ النّاسُ بِفارِغِ الصَّبْرِ لِلاِحْتِفالِ بِبُطولَتِهِ. اِحْتَشَدوا في ساحاتِ المَدينَةِ وَأَقاموا مَهْرَجانًا

كَبِيرًا تَكْرِيمًا لِلْأَمِيرِ الشُّجَاعِ. تَزَوَّجَ رامي مِنْ أَجْمَلِ الْفَتَيَاتِ فِي الْمَمْلَكَةِ وَوَرِثَ الْعَرْشَ عِنْدَمَا تُوُفِّيَ وَالِدُهُ الْمَلِكُ.

حَكَمَ الْأَمِيرُ رامي الْمَمْلَكَةَ بِحِكْمَةٍ وَعَدْلٍ، وَأَصْبَحَ مَعْرُوفًا بِشَجَاعَتِهِ وَتَضْحِيَاتِهِ مِنْ أَجْلِ شَعْبِهِ. عَاشَتِ الْمَمْلَكَةُ فِي سَلَامٍ وَازْدِهَارٍ تَحْتَ حُكْمِهِ الْعَادِلِ، وَلَمْ يُعَانُوا بَعْدَ ذَلِكَ مِنْ هَجَمَاتِ التِّنِّينِ أَوْ أَيِّ مَخَاطِرَ أُخْرَى. كَانَتْ هَذِهِ قِصَّةُ الْأَمِيرِ رامي وَالتِّنِّينِ الضَّخْمِ الَّتِي رَوَتْهَا شَهْرَزَادُ لِلْمَلِكِ شَهْرَيَارَ.

بَعْدَ سَمَاعِ الْمَلِكِ شَهْرَيَارَ لِقِصَّةِ الْأَمِيرِ رامي وَالتِّنِّينِ، أَبْدَى إِعْجَابَهُ الشَّدِيدَ بِشَجَاعَةِ الْأَمِيرِ وَحِكْمَتِهِ فِي حُكْمِ الْمَمْلَكَةِ. وَكَانَ يَتَسَاءَلُ كَيْفَ سَيَكُونُ الْأَمْرُ إِذَا كَانَ بِإِمْكَانِهِ التَّعَلُّمُ مِنْ تَجَارِبِ الْأَمِيرِ رامي وَتَطْبِيقِهَا فِي مَمْلَكَتِهِ. تَفَكَّرَ الْمَلِكُ شَهْرَيَارُ فِي مَا سَمِعَهُ مِنْ قِصَصِ شَهْرَزَادَ، وَبَدَأَ يَرَى نَفْسَهُ بِعَيْنٍ جَدِيدَةٍ.

قَرَّرَ الْمَلِكُ شَهْرَيَارُ عَدَمَ قَتْلِ شَهْرَزَادَ، لَيْسَ فَقَطْ لِأَنَّهُ كَانَ يَتَطَلَّعُ إِلَى سَمَاعِ قِصَصِهَا كُلَّ لَيْلَةٍ، وَلَكِنْ أَيْضًا لِأَنَّ قِصَصَهَا كَانَ لَهَا تَأْثِيرٌ

عَميقٌ عَلى شَخصِيَّتِهِ، وَقَد غَيَّرتهُ لِلأَفضَلِ. أَصبَحَ مَلِكًا أَكثَرَ عَدلًا وَلُطفًا بِفَضلِ تِلكَ القِصَصِ الَّتي أَلهَمَتهُ وَعَلَّمَتهُ قيمَةَ الرَّحمَةِ وَالإنصافِ.

في الأَيّامِ التّالِيَةِ، أَصبَحَ المَلِكُ شَهرَيارُ أَكثَرَ عَدلًا وَرَحمَةً في حُكمِهِ. صارَ يُنصِتُ بِعِنايَةٍ إلى شَكاوى شَعبِهِ وَيَعمَلُ بِجِدٍّ لِتَصحيحِ الظُّلمِ وَتَحسينِ حَياةِ النّاسِ. تَحَوَّلَتِ المَملَكَةُ إلى مَكانٍ أَفضَلَ لِلعَيشِ تَحتَ حُكمِ المَلِكِ شَهرَيارَ العادِلِ.

عاشَ المَلِكُ شَهرَيارُ وَشَهرَزادُ مَعًا في سَعادَةٍ وَازدِهارٍ لِسَنَواتٍ عَديدَةٍ. وَظَلَّت شَهرَزادُ تَروي القِصَصَ لِزَوجِها المَلِكِ شَهرَيارَ كُلَّ لَيلَةٍ، وَكانَت تِلكَ القِصَصُ سِرَّ سَعادَتِهِما وَسَعادَةِ مَملَكَتِهِما. وَهَكَذا انتَهَت حِكايَةُ شَهرَزادَ وَالمَلِكِ شَهرَيارَ الَّتي غَيَّرَت مَصيرَ مَملَكَةٍ بِأَكمَلِها.

Questions

1. مِمَّ كانَتِ المَمْلَكَةُ تُعاني بِسَبَبِ التِّنّينِ الضَّخْمِ؟

2. ماذا قَرَّرَ الأميرُ رامي أَنْ يَفْعَلَ عِنْدَما سَمِعَ عَنْ مُعاناةِ النّاسِ مِنَ التِّنّينِ؟

3. مِنْ أَيْنَ حَصَلَ الأميرُ رامي عَلى السِّلاحِ السِّحْرِيِّ؟

4. كَيْفَ تَمَكَّنَ الأميرُ رامي مِنْ هَزيمَةِ التِّنّينِ؟

5. كَيْفَ احْتَفَلَ النّاسُ بَعْدَ هَزيمَةِ التِّنّينِ؟

6. ما الَّذي تَساءَلَ عَنْهُ المَلِكُ شَهْرَيار بَعْدَ سَماعِ قِصَّةِ الأميرِ رامي وَالتِّنّينِ؟

7. كَيْفَ تَأَثَّرَ المَلِكُ شَهْرَيارُ بِقِصَصِ شَهْرَزاد؟

8. كَيْفَ تَغَيَّرَتِ المَمْلَكَةُ تَحْتَ حُكْمِ المَلِكِ شَهْرَيارَ؟

9. كَيْفَ أَثَّرَتْ قِصَصُ شَهْرَزادَ عَلى حَياةِ المَلِكِ شَهْرَيارَ وَشَهْرَزادَ مَعًا؟

10. كَيْفَ انْتَهَتْ حِكايَةُ شَهْرَزادَ وَالمَلِكِ شَهْرَيارَ؟

Answers

1. كانَتِ المَمْلَكَةُ تُعاني مِنْ هَجَماتٍ مُتَكَرِّرَةٍ لِلتِّنّينِ الضَّخْمِ الَّذي يُهاجِمُ القُرى وَيَخْطِفُ الشَّبابَ وَالبَناتِ الصِّغارَ لِيَأْكُلَهُمْ.

2. قَرَّرَ الأَميرُ رامي مُواجَهَةَ التِّنّينِ وَإِنْقاذَ شَعْبِهِ مِنْ هَذا الوَحْشِ المُرْعِبِ.

3. حَصَلَ الأَميرُ رامي عَلى السِّلاحِ السِّحْرِيِّ مِنْ حَكيمٍ عَجوزٍ التَقاهُ خِلالَ رِحْلَتِهِ إِلى جَبَلِ التِّنّينِ.

4. تَمَكَّنَ الأَميرُ رامي مِنْ هَزيمَةِ التِّنّينِ بِاسْتِخْدامِ السِّلاحِ السِّحْرِيِّ الَّذي أَعْطاهُ لَهُ الحَكيمُ العَجوزُ، حَيْثُ وَجَّهَ بِهِ ضَرْبَةً قاضِيَةً لِلتِّنّينِ.

5. اِحْتَفَلَ النّاسُ بَعْدَ هَزيمَةِ التِّنّينِ بِالتَّجَمُّعِ في ساحاتِ المَدينَةِ وَإِقامَةِ مَهْرَجانٍ كَبيرٍ تَكْريمًا لِلْأَميرِ الشُّجاعِ رامي.

6. تَساءَلَ المَلِكُ شَهْرَيارُ كَيْفَ سَيَكونُ الأَمْرُ إِذا كانَ بِإِمْكانِهِ التَّعَلُّمُ مِن تَجارِبِ الأَميرِ رامي وَتَطْبيقُها في مَمْلَكَتِهِ.

7. تَأَثَّرَ المَلِكُ شَهْرَيارُ بِشَكْلٍ عَميقٍ بِفَضْلِ قِصَصِ شَهْرَزادَ الَّتي أَلْهَمَتْهُ وَعَلَّمَتْهُ قيمَةَ الرَّحْمَةِ وَالإِنْصافِ، وَأَصْبَحَ مَلِكًا أَكْثَرَ عَدْلًا وَلُطْفًا.

8. تَحَوَّلَتِ المَمْلَكَةُ إِلى مَكانٍ أَفْضَلَ لِلْعَيْشِ تَحْتَ حُكْمِ المَلِكِ شَهْرَيارَ العادِلِ، حَيْثُ اسْتَمَعَ بِعِنايَةٍ إِلى شَكاوى شَعْبِهِ وَعَمِلَ بِجِدٍّ لِتَصْحيحِ الظُّلْمِ وَتَحْسينِ حَياةِ النّاسِ.

9. عاشَ المَلِكُ شَهْرَيارُ وَشَهْرَزادُ مَعًا في سَعادَةٍ وَازْدِهارٍ لِسَنَواتٍ عَديدَةٍ، وَظَلَّتْ شَهْرَزادُ تَرْوي القِصَصَ لِزَوْجِها المَلِكِ شَهْرَيارَ كُلَّ لَيْلَةٍ، وَكانَتْ تِلْكَ القِصَصُ سِرَّ سَعادَتِهِما وَسَعادَةِ مَمْلَكَتِهِما.

10. اِنْتَهَتْ حِكايَةُ شَهْرَزادَ وَالمَلِكِ شَهْرَيارَ بِتَغْييرِ مَصيرِ مَمْلَكَةٍ بِأَكْمَلِها، وَحَياتِهِما مَعًا في سَعادَةٍ وَازْدِهارٍ لِسَنَواتٍ عَديدَةٍ، حَيْثُ ظَلَّتْ شَهْرَزادُ تَرْوي القِصَصَ لِزَوْجِها المَلِكِ شَهْرَيارَ

كُلَّ لَيْلَةٍ، وَساهَمَتْ هَذِهِ القِصَصُ في تَعْزيزِ عَلاقَتِهِما وَإِحْداثِ تَغْييراتٍ إيجابِيَّةٍ عَلى مُسْتَوى المَمْلَكَةِ بِأَكْمَلِها.

Chapter 10: The Prince and the Dragon

On the next night, Scheherazade began to tell the story of the prince and the dragon to King Shahryar.

In a faraway kingdom, there was a young and brave prince named Rami. The kingdom suffered from frequent attacks by a huge dragon that lived in a nearby mountain. The dragon would attack the villages and kidnap young boys and girls to eat them. The people lived in constant fear and did not dare to confront the giant dragon.

One day, Prince Rami met a man from one of the devastated villages. The man said to him, "Oh, our prince, the dragon has kidnapped my little daughter, and we live in unbearable fear. I beg you to save us from this terrifying monster."

Prince Rami decided to face the dragon and save his people from this terrifying creature. He prepared himself with the best weapons and armor and set out on his journey to the dragon's mountain. During his journey, he met a wise old man who gave him a magic weapon that could defeat the dragon. The wise man said to the prince, "Use this magic weapon carefully, for it is the only one that can defeat the giant dragon."

Prince Rami reached the dragon's mountain and found the huge monster sleeping. He decided to wait until the dragon woke up to face him bravely. When the dragon woke up,

Prince Rami shouted, "Oh, evil dragon, today I will kill you and save my people from your brutal attacks!"

He prepared to face the dragon and used the magic weapon given to him by the wise old man. The battle began between Prince Rami and the huge dragon. The dragon flapped its wings and breathed fire at the prince while Rami dodged skillfully and used his magic weapon to strike hard blows at the dragon. The battle continued for hours, and Prince Rami was slowly losing his energy.

In a decisive moment, Rami summoned all his courage and remaining strength and managed to deliver a fatal blow to the dragon using his magic weapon. The dragon fell to the ground and breathed its last breath, and thus, Prince Rami saved his people from the terrifying monster.

Prince Rami returned to the kingdom, where people awaited him eagerly to celebrate his bravery. They gathered in the city squares and held a big festival in honor of the brave prince. Rami married one of the most beautiful girls in the kingdom and inherited the throne when his father, the king, died.

Prince Rami ruled the kingdom wisely and fairly and became known for his courage and sacrifices for his people. The kingdom lived in peace and prosperity under his fair rule and did not suffer any more dragon attacks or other risks. This was the story of Prince Rami and the huge dragon told by Scheherazade to King Shahryar.

After hearing the story of Prince Rami and the dragon, King Shahryar expressed his deep admiration for the prince's bravery and wisdom in ruling his kingdom. He wondered what it would be like if he could learn from Prince Rami's experiences and apply them to his own kingdom. King Shahryar reflected on the stories he had heard from Scheherazade and began to see himself in a new light.

King Shahryar decided not to kill Scheherazade not only because he looked forward to hearing her stories every night, but also because her stories had a profound effect on his personality and had changed him for the better. He became a more just and kind king thanks to those stories that inspired him and taught him the value of mercy and fairness.

In the following days, King Shahryar became more just and merciful in his rule. He listened carefully to his people's complaints and worked hard to correct the injustice and improve people's lives. The kingdom turned into a better place to live under King Shahryar's fair rule.

King Shahryar and Scheherazade lived together in happiness and prosperity for many years. Scheherazade continued to tell stories to her husband, King Shahryar, every night, and those stories were the secret to their happiness and the happiness of their kingdom. And thus ended the story of Scheherazade and King Shahryar, which changed the fate of the entire kingdom.

Questions

1. What was the kingdom suffering from because of the giant dragon?
2. What did Prince Rami decide when he heard about the people's suffering from the dragon?
3. Where did Prince Rami get the magical weapon from?
4. How did Prince Rami manage to defeat the dragon?
5. How did the people celebrate after defeating the dragon?
6. What did King Shahryar wonder about after hearing the story of Prince Rami and the dragon?
7. How was King Shahryar affected by the stories of Scheherazade?
8. How did the kingdom change under King Shahryar's rule?
9. How did the stories of Scheherazade affect the lives of King Shahryar and Scheherazade together?
10. How did the story of Scheherazade and King Shahryar end?

Answers

1. The kingdom was suffering from frequent attacks by the giant dragon that would attack villages and kidnap young boys and girls to eat them.

2. Prince Rami decided to confront the dragon and save his people from this terrifying monster.

3. Prince Rami obtained the magical weapon from a wise old man he met during his journey to the dragon mountain.

4. Prince Rami managed to defeat the dragon by using the magical weapon given to him by the wise old man and delivering a fatal blow to the dragon.

5. The people celebrated after defeating the dragon by gathering in the city squares and holding a big festival to honor the brave Prince Rami.

6. King Shahryar wondered how it would be if he could learn from Prince Rami's experiences and apply them in his own kingdom.

7. King Shahryar was deeply influenced by the stories of Scheherazade, which inspired him and taught him the value of mercy and justice, and he became a more just and kind king.

8. The kingdom became a better place to live under the rule of the just King Shahryar, who listened carefully

to the complaints of his people and worked hard to correct injustices and improve their lives.

9. King Shahryar and Scheherazade lived together in happiness and prosperity for many years, with Scheherazade continuing to tell stories to her husband every night, and those stories were the secret of their happiness and the happiness of their kingdom.

10. The story of Scheherazade and King Shahryar ended with the change of the fate of the entire kingdom and making them live together in happiness and prosperity for many years, with Scheherazade continuing to tell stories to her husband every night, and these stories helped to strengthen their bond and bring about positive changes throughout the kingdom.

lingualism

Visit our website for information on current and upcoming titles and free language learning resources.

www.lingualism.com

www.ingramcontent.com/pod-product-compliance
Lightning Source LLC
Chambersburg PA
CBHW070150080526
44586CB00015B/1927